Washington Nationals 2019

A Baseball Companion

Edited by Patrick Dubuque, Aaron Gleeman and Bret Sayre

Baseball Prospectus

Craig Brown and Dave Pease, Consultant Editors
Rob McQuown and Harry Pavlidis, Statistics Editors

Copyright © 2019 by DIY Baseball, LLC.
All rights reserved

This book or any part thereof may not be reproduced or transmitted in any form or by any means, electronic or mechanical, including photocopying, recording, or by any information storage and retrieval system, without permission in writing from the publisher.

Limit of Liability/Disclaimer of Warranty: While the publisher and the author have used their best efforts in preparing this book, they make no representations or warranties with respect to the accuracy or completeness of the contents of this book and specifically disclaim any implied warranties of merchantability or fitness for a particular purpose. No warranty may be created or extended by sales representatives or written sales materials. The advice and strategies contained herein may not be suitable for your situation. You should consult with a professional where appropriate. Neither the publisher nor the author shall be liable for any loss of profit or any other commercial damages, including but not limited to special, incidental, consequential, or other damages.

Library of Congress Cataloging-in-Publication Data:
paperback
ISBN-13: 978-1-949332-58-2

Project Credits
Cover Design: Kathleen Dyson
Interior Design and Production: Jeff Pease, Dave Pease
Layout: Jeff Pease, Dave Pease

Baseball icon courtesy of Uberux, from https://www.shareicon.net/author/uberux

Ballpark diagram courtesy of Lou Spirito/THIRTY81 Project, https://thirty81project.com/

Manufactured in the United States of America
10 9 8 7 6 5 4 3 2 1

Table of Contents

Foreword v
    Rob Mains

Statistical Introduction vii

Part 1: Team Analysis

Table for Two: Previewing the 2019 Washington Nationals 3
    Sydney Bergman and Patrick Dubuque

Performance Graphs 9

2018 Team Performance 10

2019 Team Projections 11

Team Personnel 12

Nationals Park Stats 13

Nationals Team Analysis 15

Part 2: Player Analysis

Nationals Player Analysis 20

Nationals Prospects 97

Part 3: Featured Articles

The Hole in The Shift is Fixing Itself 109
    Russell Carleton

The State of the Quality Start 113
    Rob Mains

Heads-Up Hacking—The First Pitch 119
    Matthew Trueblood

A Hymn for the Index Stat 125
    Patrick Dubuque

Index of Names 129

Foreword

Rob Mains

Welcome to this companion of the 2019 Washington Nationals. We at Baseball Prospectus are excited to provide this analysis of the Nationals.

Our website, Baseball Prospectus, is a leader in delivering high-quality commentary and data to baseball fans everywhere. To some, those words—commentary and data—appear mutually exclusive. There are people out there who believe that traditional analysis and advanced analytics must run on different paths. But the simplistic narrative of stats vs. traditionalists just isn't true. Every team's analytics department interacts with scouting, development, and major league operations with a common goal: Delivering a championship. New technologies, like radar tracking of pitch speeds and movement, enable talent evaluators to focus on qualitative aspects of pitching like mechanics and pitch sequencing. In-game strategies like infield shifts, based on batters' hit tendencies, help turn balls in play into outs. Hitters use information to adjust their swings to maximize run production.

All these numbers can seem, at best, intimidating, and at worst, counterproductive to the casual fan. Even as technology and analysis have embedded themselves deeply into the way teams run, it can often feel like statistics create a displacement between the viewer and the sport, breaking them out of the action. And yet every fan incorporates the numbers to some degree; stats like batting average and earned run average, so fundamental to how we talk about performance, are actually complicated formulas. They don't bother people because those formulas have become second nature, as easy to translate as the action on the field.

Along the way, new statistics have entered baseball's lexicon. You'll see some of them, like on-base percentage (which measures a batter's ability to get on base via walk, hit batter, or hit), OPS (on-base plus slugging), and average exit velocity (the speed of balls off a hitter's bat) on broadcasts. Others, like DRC+, might well be new to you. Some of them have been well-defined to the public, others haven't. That lack of context has created ambiguity. Fans know that a ball hit 100 mph is scorched, but does that mean extra bases? (Not if it's hit on the ground or high in the air it doesn't.)

For those who are amenable to them, the new statistics can increase the enjoyment and understanding of the game. They can help fans identify when a pitcher is tiring, when a stolen base or a bunt attempt makes sense (and, more often, when it doesn't), or how a team's lineup might be constructed. Websites like Baseball Prospectus add to that understanding by weaving metrics into the narrative of the game. That's the goal of this publication: to take some of the newer, more complicated statistics and make them as intuitive as the ones on the back of old baseball cards.

But you don't need to love analytics to love baseball. The fans at BP who worked together to write this guide are captivated first and foremost by the game itself. We're drawn to Aaron Judge's power, Francisco Lindor's glove, Billy Hamilton's speed and Patrick Corbin's slider and don't need numbers to tell us why they're so mesmerizing. The underlying statistics provide depth to the game that we all love.

We hope you'll find that this guide helps you better understand the Nationals. Our analysts have studied the team's major league personnel and its minor league affiliates to identify their strengths and weaknesses, both the obvious ones and those that only a careful dissection of players' performances—yes, including the data—can reveal. You don't need us to tell you who was good and who wasn't in 2018, but our models and writers can help you project how each player is going to perform this year and beyond, and appreciate the greatness of each new game as it unfolds. As in the sport itself, the human and analytic components combine to generate a deeper overall understanding.

Think back to the first time you saw a baseball game on a high-definition TV. You'd grown familiar with how the game looked and felt on a picture tube. But new TV allowed you to see details that you'd never seen before. That's how advanced statistics work. The game itself is why you're here and why you're buying this. (And, for that matter, why we wrote it.) The statistical measures provide the sharper focus, the detail, the depth of knowledge that you didn't have before, generating an overall superior picture. Enjoy the view.

—*Rob Mains is an author of Baseball Prospectus.*

Statistical Introduction

Sports are, fundamentally, a blend of athletic endeavor and storytelling. Baseball, like any other sport, tells its stories in so many ways: in the arc of a game from the stands or a season from the box scores, in photos, or even in numbers. At Baseball Prospectus, we understand that statistics don't replace observation or any of baseball's stories, but complement everything else that makes the game so much fun.

What stats help us with is with patterns and precision, variance and value. This book can help you learn things you may not see from watching a game or hundred, whether it's the path of a career over time or the breadth of the entire MLB. We'd also never ask you to choose between our numbers and the experience of viewing a game from the cheap seats or the comfort of your home; our publication combines running the numbers with observations and wisdom from some of the brightest minds we can find. But if you *do* want to learn more about the numbers beyond what's on the backs of player jerseys, let us help explain.

Offense

At the end of this past year, we've revised our methodology for determining batting value. Long-time readers of Baseball Prospectus will notice that we've retired True Average in favor of a new metric: Deserved Runs Created Plus (DRC+). Developed by Jonathan Judge and our stats team, this statistic measures everything a player does at the plate–reaching base, hitting for power, making outs, and moving runners over–and puts it on a scale where 100 equals league-average performance. A DRC+ of 150 is terrific, a DRC+ of 100 is average, and a DRC+ of 75 means you better be an excellent defender.

DRC+ also does a better job than any of our previous metrics in taking contextual factors into account. The model adjusts for how the park affects performance, but also for things like the talent of the opposing pitcher, value of different types of batted-ball events, league, temperature, and other factors. It's able to describe a player's expected offensive contribution than any other statistic we've found over the years, and also does a better job of predicting future performance as well.

The other aspect of run-scoring is baserunning, which we quantify using Baserunning Runs. BRR not only records the value of stolen bases (or getting caught in the act), but also accounts for a runner's ability to go first to third on a single or advance on a fly ball.

Defense

Where offensive value is *relatively* easy to identify and understand, defensive value is ... not. Over the past dozen years, the sabermetric community has focused mostly on stats based on zone data: a real-live human person records the type of batted ball and estimated landing location, and models are created that give expected outs. From there, you can compare fielders' actual outs to those expected ones. Simple, right?

Unfortunately, zone data has two major issues. First, zone data is recorded by commercial data providers who keep the raw data private unless you pay for it. (All the statistics we build in this book and on our website use public data as inputs.) That hurts our ability to test assumptions or duplicate results. Second, over the years it has become apparent that there's quite a bit of "noise" in zone-based fielding analysis. Sometimes the conclusions drawn from zone data don't hold up to scrutiny, and sometimes the different data provided by different providers don't look anything alike, giving wildly different results. Sometimes the hard-working professional stringers or scorers might unknowingly inflict unconscious bias into the mix: for example good fielders will often be credited with more expected outs despite the data, and ballparks with high press boxes tend to score more line drives than ones with a lower press box.

Enter our Fielding Runs Above Average (FRAA). For most positions, FRAA is built from play-by-play data, which allows us to avoid the subjectivity found in many other fielding metrics. The idea is this: count how many fielding plays are made by a given player and compare that to expected plays for an average fielder at their position (based on pitcher ground-ball tendencies and batter handedness). Then we adjust for park and base-out situations.

When it comes to catchers, our methodology is a little different thanks to the laundry list of responsibilities they're tasked with beyond just, well, catching and throwing the ball. By now you've probably heard about "framing" or the art of making umpires more likely to call balls outside the strike zone for strikes. To put this into one tidy number, we incorporate pitch tracking data (for the years it exists) and adjust for important factors like pitcher, umpire, batter, and home-field advantage using a mixed-model approach. This grants us a number for how many strikes the catcher is personally adding to (or subtracting from) his pitchers' performance ... which we then convert to runs added or lost using linear weights.

Framing is one of the biggest parts of determining catcher value, but we also take into account blocking balls from going past, whether a scorer deems it a passed ball or a wild pitch. We use a similar approach–one that really benefits from the pitch tracking data that tells us what ends up in the dirt and what doesn't. We also include a catcher's ability to prevent stolen bases and how well they field balls in play, and *finally* we come up with our FRAA for catchers.

Pitching

Both pitching and fielding make up the half of baseball that isn't run scoring: run prevention. Separating pitching from fielding is a tough task, and most recent pitching analysis has branched off from Voros McCracken's famous (and controversial) statement, "There is little if any difference among major-league pitchers in their ability to prevent hits on balls hit in the field of play." The research of the analytic community has validated this to some extent, and there are a host of "defense-independent" pitching measures that have been developed to try and extricate the effect of the defense behind a hurler from the pitcher's work.

Our solution to this quandry is Deserved Run Average (DRA), our core pitching metric. DRA looks like earned run average (ERA), the tried-and-true pitching stat you've seen on every baseball broadcast or box score from the past century, but it's very different. To start, DRA takes an event-by-event look at what the pitchers does, and adjusts the value of that event based on different environmental factors like park, batter, catcher, umpire, base-out situation, run differential, inning, defense, home field advantage, pitcher role, and temperature. That mixed model gives us a pitcher's expected contribution, similar to what we do for our DRC+ model for hitters and FRAA model for catchers. (Oh, and we also consider the pitcher's effect on basestealing and on balls getting past the catcher.)

It's important to note that DRA is set to the scale of runs allowed per nine innings (RA9) instead of ERA, which makes DRA's scale slightly higher than ERA's. The reason for this is because ERA tends to overrate three types of pitchers:

1. Pitchers who play in parks where scorers hand out more errors. Official scorers differ significantly in the frequency at which they assign errors to fielders.
2. Ground-ball pitchers, because a substantial proportion of errors occur on grounders.
3. Pitchers who aren't very good. Better pitchers often allow fewer unearned runs than bad pitchers, because good pitchers tend to find ways to get out of jams.

Since the last time you picked up an edition of this book, we've also made a few minor changes to DRA to make it better. Recent research into "tunneling"–the act of throwing consecutive pitches that appear similar from a batter's point of view until after the swing decision point–data has given us a new contextual factor to account for in DRA: plate distance. This refers to the distance between successive pitches as they approach the plate, and while it has a smaller effect than factors like velocity or whiff rate, it still can help explain pitcher strikeout rate in our model.

New Pitching Metrics for 2019

We're including a few "new" pitching metrics for 2019's suite of Baseball Prospectus publications, but you may be familiar with them if you've spent time scouring the internet for stats.

Fastball Percentage

Our fastball percentage (FB%) statistic measures how frequently a pitcher throws a pitch classified as a "fastball," measured as a percentage of overall pitches thrown. We qualify three types of fastballs:

1. The traditional four-seam fastball;
2. The two-seam fastball or sinker;
3. "Hard cutters," which are pitches that have the movement profile of a cut fastball and are used as the pitcher's primary offering or in place of a more traditional fastball.

For example, a pitcher with a FB% of 67 throws any combination of these three pitches about two-thirds of the time.

Whiff Rate

Everybody loves a swing and a miss, and whiff rate (WHF) measures how frequently pitchers induce a swinging strike. To calculate WHF, we add up all the pitches thrown that ended with a swinging strike, then divide that number by a pitcher's total pitches thrown. Most often, high whiff rates correlate with high strikeout rates (and overall effective pitcher performance).

Called Strike Probability

Called Strike Probability (CSP) is a number that represents the likelihood that all of a pitcher's pitches will be called a strike while controlling for location, pitcher and batter handedness, umpire and count. Here's how it works: on each pitch, our model determines how many times (out of 100) that a similar pitch was called for a strike given those factors mentioned above, and when normalized for each batter's strike zone. Then we average the CSP for all pitches thrown by a pitcher in a season, and that gives us the yearly CSP percentage you see in the stats boxes.

As you might imagine, pitchers with a higher CSP are more likely to work in the zone, where pitchers with a lower CSP are likely locating their pitches outside the normal strike zone, for better or for worse.

Projections

Many of you aren't turning to this book just for a look at what a player has done, but for a look at what a player is going to do: the PECOTA projections. PECOTA, initially developed by Nate Silver (who has moved on to greater fame as a political analyst), consists of three parts:

1. Major-league equivalencies, which use minor-league statistics to project how a player will perform in the major leagues;
2. Baseline forecasts, which use weighted averages and regression to the mean to estimate a player's current true talent level; and
3. Aging curves, which uses the career paths of comparable players to estimate how a player's statistics are likely to change over time.

With all those important things covered, let's take a look at what's in the book this year.

Team Prospectus

You bought this book to learn more about your favorite (or maybe least-favorite, who are we to judge?) team, so let's talk about them. After a thoughtful preview of the 2019 season, you'll be presented with our Team Prospectus. This outlines many of the key statistics for each team's 2018 season, as well as a very inviting stadium diagram.

First you'll find the Performance Graphs page. The first is the 2018 Hit List Ranking. This shows our Hit List Rank for the team on each day of the 2018 season and is intended to give you a picture of the ups and downs of the team's season, including their highest and lowest ranks of the year. Hit List Rank measures overall team performance and drives the Hit List Power Rankings at the baseballprospectus.com website.

The second graph is Committed Payroll and helps you see how the team's payroll has compared to the MLB and divisional average payrolls over time. Payroll figures are currents as of January 1, 2019; with so many free agents still unsigned as of this writing, the final 2018 figure will likely be significantly different for many teams. (In the meantime, you can always find the most current data at Baseball Prospectus' Cot's Baseball Contracts page.)

Washington Nationals 2019

The third graph is Farm System Ranking and displays how the Baseball Prospectus prospect team has ranked the organization's farm system since 2007. It also indicates the highest and lowest ranks that the farm system achieved over that time.

We start the Team Performance page with the squad's unadjusted and third-order 2018 win-loss records, presented in divisional context. We then list the three highest performing hitters and pitchers by WARP for 2018. Beneath that are a host of other team statistics. **Pythag** presents an adjusted 2018 winning percentage, calculated by taking runs scored per game (**RS/G**) and runs allowed per game (**RA/G**) for the team, and running them through a version of Bill James' Pythagorean formula that was refined and improved by David Smyth and Brandon Heipp. (The formula is called "Pythagenpat," which is equally fun to type and to say.)

Next up is **DRC+**, described earlier, to indicate the overall hitting ability of the team either above or below league-average. Run prevention on the pitching side is covered by **DRA** (also mentioned earlier) and another metric: Fielding Independent Pitching (**FIP**), which calculates another ERA-like statistic based on strikeouts, walks, and home runs recorded. Defensive Efficiency Rating (**DER**) tells us the percentage of balls in play turned into outs for the team, and is a quick fielding shorthand that rounds out run prevention.

After that, we have several measures related to roster composition, as opposed to on-field performance. **B-Age** and **P-Age** tell us the average age of a team's batters and pitchers, respectively. **Salary** is the combined team payroll for all on-field players, and Doug Pappas' Marginal Dollars per Marginal Win (**M$/MW**) tells us how much money a team spent to earn production above replacement level.

Ending this batch of statistics is the number of disabled list days a team had over the season (**DL Days**) and the amount of salary paid to players on the disabled list (**$ on DL**); this final number is expressed as a percentage of total payroll.

Next to each of these stats, we've listed each team's MLB rank in that category from 1st to 30th. In this, 1st always indicates a positive outcome and 30th a negative outcome, except in the case of salary–1st is highest.

The Team Projections page is intended to convey the team's operational capacity entering the 2019 season. We start with the team's PECOTA projected record for 2019, again in divisional context. The **+/-** column indicates how many more or less wins the team is projected to get than they got in 2018. We then list the three highest projected hitters and pitchers by WARP for 2018. A brief farm system summary follows, with the team's top prospect and number of BP Top 101 Prospects. Finally, we list the key new players and departed players, along with their 2019 projected WARP.

Alex Bregman 3B

Born: 03/30/94 Age: 25 Bats: R Throws: R
Height: 6'0" Weight: 180 Origin: Round 1, 2015 Draft (#2 overall)

YEAR	TEAM	LVL	AGE	PA	R	2B	3B	HR	RBI	BB	K	SB	CS	AVG/OBP/SLG
2016	CCH	AA	22	285	54	16	2	14	46	42	26	5	3	.297/.415/.559
2016	FRE	AAA	22	83	17	6	0	6	15	5	12	2	1	.333/.373/.641
2016	HOU	MLB	22	217	31	13	3	8	34	15	52	2	0	.264/.313/.478
2017	HOU	MLB	23	626	88	39	5	19	71	55	97	17	5	.284/.352/.475
2018	HOU	MLB	24	705	105	51	1	31	103	96	85	10	4	.286/.394/.532
2019	HOU	MLB	25	675	96	38	3	23	78	73	107	12	4	.272/.359/.463

Breakout: 6% Improve: 52% Collapse: 5% Attrition: 2% MLB: 100%
Comparables: Anthony Rendon, David Wright, Pablo Sandoval

YEAR	TEAM	LVL	AGE	PA	DRC+	VORP	BABIP	BRR	FRAA	WARP
2016	CCH	AA	22	285	172	38.9	.286	1.6	SS(51): -3.4, 3B(11): 1.4	2.7
2016	FRE	AAA	22	83	161	10.0	.333	-1.2	SS(14): 2.1, LF(3): -0.1	0.8
2016	HOU	MLB	22	217	107	9.6	.317	0.5	3B(40): 0.9, SS(6): -0.1	1.1
2017	HOU	MLB	23	626	114	34.7	.311	-1.5	3B(132): 8.7, SS(30): -2.9	3.9
2018	HOU	MLB	24	705	150	72.6	.289	-1.6	3B(136): 5.4, SS(28): -0.4	7.4
2019	HOU	MLB	25	675	125	37.3	.295	0.0	3B 7, SS 0	4.6

After the projections page, we share a few items about the team's home ballpark. There's the aforementioned diagram of the park's dimensions (including distances to the outfield wall), a few important biographical facts about the stadium, a graphic showing the height of the wall from the left-field pole to the right-field pole, and a table showing three-year park factors for the stadium. The park factors are displayed as indexes where 100 is average, 110 means that the park inflates the statistic in question by 10 percent, and 90 means that the park deflates the statistic in question by 10 percent.

Following the ballpark page, we have a **Personnel** section that lists many of the important decision-makers and upper-level field and operations staff members for the franchise, as well as any former Baseball Prospectus staff members who are currently part of the organization.

Position Players

After all that information and a thoughtful bylined essay covering each team, we present our player comments. Each player is listed with the major-league team who employed him as of early January 2019. If a player changed teams after that point via free agency, trade, or any other method, you'll be able to find them in the book for their previous squad.

First, we cover biographical information (age is as of June 30, 2019) before moving onto the stats themselves. Our statistic columns include standard identifying information like **YEAR**, **TEAM**, **LVL** (level of affiliated play) and **AGE** before getting into the numbers. Next, we provide raw, unstranslated numbers like you might find on the back of your dad's baseball cards: **PA** (plate appearances), **R** (runs), **2B** (doubles), **3B** (triples), **HR** (home runs), **RBI** (runs batted in), **BB** (walks), **K** (strikeouts), **SB** (stolen bases) and **CS** (caught stealing). Then we have unadjusted "slash" statistics: **AVG** (batting average), **OBP** (on-base percentage) and **SLG** (slugging percentage).

Just below the stats box is **PECOTA** data, which is discussed further in a following section. After that, it's on to a pithy and always-informative comment written by a member of the Baseball Prospectus staff, before we cover more stats.

The second text box repeats YEAR, TEAM, LVL, AGE, and PA, then moves on to **DRC+** (Deserved Runs Created Plus), which we described earlier as total offensive expected contribution compared to the league average. Next, one of our oldest active metrics, **VORP** (Value Over Replacement Player), considers offensive production, position and plate appearances. In essence, it is the number of runs contributed beyond what a replacement-level player at the same position would contribute if given the same percentage of team plate appearances. VORP does not consider the quality of a player's defense.

BABIP (batting average on balls in play) tells us how often a ball in play fell for a hit, and can help us identify whether a batter may have been lucky or not … but note that high BABIPs also tend to follow the great hitters of our time, as well as speedy singles hitters who put the ball on the ground.

The next item is **BRR** (Baserunning Runs), which covers all of a player's baserunning accomplishments which includes (but isn't limited to) swiped bags and failed attempts. Next is **FRAA** (Fielding Runs Above Average), which also includes the number of games previously played at each position noted in parentheses. Multi-position players have only their two most frequent positions listed here, but their total FRAA number reflects all positions played.

Our last column here is **WARP** (Wins Above Replacement Player). WARP estimates the total value of a player, which means for hitters it takes into account hitting runs above average (calculated using the DRC+ model), BRR and FRAA. Then, it makes an adjustment for positions played and gives the player a credit for plate appearances based upon the difference between "replacement level"¬–which is derived from the quality of players added to a team's roster after the start of the season¬–and the league average.

Catchers

Catchers are a special breed, and thus they have earned their own separate box which displays some of the defensive metrics that we've built just for them. As an example, let's check out J.T. Realmuto.

YEAR	TEAM	P. COUNT	FRM RUNS	BLK RUNS	THRW RUNS	TOT RUNS
2016	MIA	18935	-8.5	1.8	2.1	-5.6
2017	MIA	18959	5.3	1.7	1.0	9.1
2018	MIA	16399	-0.4	0.9	0.1	0.4
2019	PHI	18448	-1.4	1.5	0.7	0.8

The **YEAR** and **TEAM** columns match what you'd find in the other stat box. **P. COUNT** indicates the number of pitches thrown while the catcher was behind the plate, including swinging strikes, fouls, and balls in play. **FRM RUNS** is the total run value the catcher provided (or cost) his team by influencing the umpire to call strikes where other catchers did not. **BLK RUNS** expresses the total run value above or below average for the catcher's ability to prevent wild pitches and passed balls. **THRW RUNS** is calculated using a similar model as the previous two statistics, and it measures a catcher's ability to throw out basestealers but also to dissuade them from testing his arm in the first place. It takes into account factors like the pitcher (including his delivery and pickoff move) and baserunner (who could be as fast as Billy Hamilton or as slow as Yonder Alonso). **TOT RUNS** is the sum of all of the previous three statistics.

Pitchers

Let's give our pitchers a turn, using 2018 NL Cy Young winner Jacob deGrom as our example. Take a look at his first stat block: the first line and the **YEAR**, **TEAM**, **LVL** and **AGE** columns are the same as in the position player example earlier.

Here too, we have a series of columns that display raw, unadjusted statistics compiled by the pitcher over the course of a season: **W** (wins), **L** (losses), **SV** (saves), **G** (games pitched), **GS** (games started), **IP** (innings pitched), **H** (hits allowed) and **HR** (home runs allowed). Next we have two statistics that are rates: **BB/9** (walks per nine innings) and **K/9** (strikeouts per nine innings), before returning to the unadjusted **K** (strikeouts).

Next up is **GB%** (ground ball percentage), which is the percentage of all batted balls that were hit in the ground, including both outs and hits. Remember, this is based on observational data and subject to human error, so please approach this with a healthy dose of skepticism.

BABIP (batting average on balls in play) is calculated using the same methodology as it is for position players, but it often tells us more about a pitcher than it does a hitter. With pitchers, a high BABIP is often due to poor defense or bad luck, and can often be an indicator of potential rebound, and a low BABIP may be cause to expect performance regression. (A typical league-average BABIP is close to .290-.300.)

After a witty 150ish words on the player like only Baseball Prospectus's staff can provide, it's on to that second stat block, which repeats the YEAR, TEAM, LVL, and AGE columns. The metrics **WHIP** (walks plus hits per inning pitched) and **ERA**

Washington Nationals 2019

(earned run average) are old standbys: WHIP measures walks and hits allowed on a per-inning basis, while ERA measures earned runs on a nine-inning basis. Neither of these stats are translated or adjusted.

DRA (Deserved Run Average) was described at length earlier, and measures how many runs the pitcher "deserved" to allow per nine innings. Please note that since we lack all the data points that would make for a "real" DRA for minor-league events, the DRA displayed for minor league partial-seasons is based off of different data. (That data is a modified version of our cFIP metric, which you can find more information about on our website.)

Jacob deGrom   RHP
Born: 06/19/88   Age: 31   Bats: L   Throws: R
Height: 6'4"   Weight: 180   Origin: Round 9, 2010 Draft (#272 overall)

YEAR	TEAM	LVL	AGE	W	L	SV	G	GS	IP	H	HR	BB/9	K/9	K	GB%	BABIP
2016	NYN	MLB	28	7	8	0	24	24	148	142	15	2.2	8.7	143	47%	.312
2017	NYN	MLB	29	15	10	0	31	31	201[1]	180	28	2.6	10.7	239	48%	.305
2018	NYN	MLB	30	10	9	0	32	32	217	152	10	1.9	11.2	269	48%	.281
2019	NYN	MLB	31	13	9	0	31	31	186	145	18	2.3	10.7	221	46%	.286

Breakout: 8%   Improve: 29%   Collapse: 28%   Attrition: 6%   MLB: 85%
Comparables: Erik Bedard, A.J. Burnett, CC Sabathia

YEAR	TEAM	LVL	AGE	WHIP	ERA	DRA	WARP	MPH	FB%	WHF	CSP
2016	NYN	MLB	28	1.20	3.04	3.30	3.5	96.3	59.6	12.1	47.2
2017	NYN	MLB	29	1.19	3.53	3.02	5.7	97.2	55.5	14.5	49.5
2018	NYN	MLB	30	0.91	1.70	2.09	8.0	98.2	52.1	16.3	48.4
2019	NYN	MLB	31	1.02	2.91	3.23	3.9	96.6	54.5	14.8	48.2

Just like with hitters, **WARP** (Wins Above Replacement Player) is a total value metric that puts pitchers of all stripes on the same scale as position players. We use DRA as the primary input for our calculation of WARP. You might notice that relief pitchers (due to their limited innings) may have a lower WARP than you were expecting or than you might see in other WARP-like metrics. WARP does not take leverage into account, just the actions a pitcher performs and the expected value of those actions ... which ends up judging high-leverage relief pitchers differently than you might imagine given their prestige and market value.

MPH gives you the pitcher's 95th percentile velocity for the noted season, in order to give you an idea of what the *peak* fastball velocity a pitcher possesses. Since this comes from our pitch tracking data, it is not publicly available for minor-league pitchers.

Finally, we display the three new pitching metrics we described earlier. **FB%** (fastball percentage) gives you the percentage of fastballs thrown out of all pitches. **WhiffRt** (whiff rate) tells you the percentage of swinging strikes induced out of all pitches. **CS Prob** (called strike probability) expresses the likelihood of all pitches thrown to result in a called strike, after controlling for factors like handedness, umpire, pitch type, count, and location.

PECOTA

All players have PECOTA projections for 2019, as well as a set of other numbers that describe the performance of comparable players according to PECOTA. All projections for 2019 are for the player at the date we went to press in early January and are projected into the league and park context as indicated by the team abbreviation. All PECOTA projected statistics represent a player's projected major-league performance.

The numbers beneath the player's stats–Breakout, Improve, Collapse, Attrition–are part and parcel of the PECOTA projections. They estimate the likelihood of changes in performance relative to the player's previously-established level of production, based on the performance of comparable players:

Breakout Rate is the percent change that a player's production will improve by at least 20 percent relative to the weighted average of his performance over his most recent seasons.

Improve Rate is the percent chance that a player's production will improve at all relative to his baseline performance. A player who is expected to perform just the same as he has in the recent past will have an Improve Rate of 50 percent.

Collapse Rate is the percent chance that a position player's production will decline by at least 25 percent relative to his baseline performance.

Attrition Rate operates on playing time rather than performance. Specifically, it measures the likelihood that a player's playing time will decrease by at least 50 percent relative to his established level.

Breakout Rate and Collapse Rate can sometimes be counterintuitive for players who have already experienced a radical change in performance level. It's also worth noting that the projected decline in a player's rate performances might not be indicative of an expected decline in underlying ability or skill, but could just be an anticipated correction following a breakout season.

MLB% is the percentage of similar players who played in the major leagues in their relevant season.

The final pieces of information are the player's three highest-scoring comparable players as determined by PECOTA. All comparables represent a snapshot of how the listed player was performing at the same age as the current player, so if a 23-year-old pitcher is compared to Bartolo Colon, he's actually being compared to a 23-year-old Colon, not the version that pitched for the Rangers in 2018, nor to Colon's career as a whole.

Washington Nationals 2019

A few points about pitcher projections. First, we aren't yet projecting peak velocity, so that column will be blank in the PECOTA lines. Second, projecting DRA is trickier than evaluating past performance, because it is unclear how deserving each pitcher will be of his anticipated outcomes. However, we know that another DRA-related statistic–contextual FIP or cFIP–estimates future run scoring very well. So for PECOTA, the projected DRA figures you see are based on the past cFIPs generated by the pitcher and comparable players over time, along with the other factors described above.

Lineouts

In each chapter's Lineouts section, you'll find abbreviated text comments, as well as most of same information you'd find in our full player comments. We limit the stats boxes in this section to only including the 2018 information for each player.

Exclusive Player Visualizations

In our constant battle to provide you with new and interesting baseball content you can't find anywhere else, we've added a trio of data visualizations to each hitter's entry in these books and a pair of visualizations for each pitcher.

For hitters, you'll find three new infographics. The first is each player's **Batted Ball Distribution**, which displays the five major sections of the field: LF (left), LCF (left center), CF (center), RCF (right center), and RF (right). The percentage indicated tells us what percentage of batted balls from that hitter fell within that part of the field during the 2018 season. We've also included the hitter's slugging percentage on balls in play (also called **SLGCON**) for that part of the field.

You'll also see two heatmaps: **Strike Zone vs LHP** and **Strike Zone vs RHP**. These heat maps represent a view of the strike zone from behind the catcher. Areas where there is a darker coloration represent the places where a higher percentage of pitches resulted in hits. In other words, the heatmap represents a hitter's "sweet spots" for getting hits against either left-handed or right-handed pitchers, depending on the image.

Pitchers get two images that help explain what their pitches look like from a hitter's perspective: **Pitch Shape vs LHH** and **Pitch Shape vs RHH**. These images show you the shape and the "tunneling" effect of each pitcher's offerings from the batter's perspective. For each type of pitch that a pitcher throws (represented by an indicator shape), there's a set of dots indicating the flight path, where each dot represents a 0.01-second interval. This maps the average trajectory and speed of an offering, ending where the ball crosses the plate. The solid black box represents the regular strike zone, while the gray contour lines indicate the range of locations that a pitcher typically works in.

Below the image, we provide a bit more detailed information about each pitcher's average offering in the **Pitch Types** box. Here, we also list each of the pitcher's major offerings under the **Type** column.

- **Fastballs** (which usually refers to the four-seam variation)
- **Sinkers** and/or two-seam fastballs
- **Cutters** (which could include "hard" cutters like cut fastballs and "soft" cutters that resemble hard sliders)
- **Changeups** (not including most splitters)
- **Splitters** (split-fingered pitches, forkballs, and some split-changes)
- **Sliders** and/or slurves
- **Curveballs** (including spike-curveballs and knuckle-curveballs, as well as some slurvy curves)
- **Slow curveballs** and/or eephus pitches
- **Knuckleballs**
- **Screwballs**

The **Freq** column indicates the percentage of overall pitches that fall into each of those type categories; if a pitcher has a 16.55% score for changeups, then that's the percent of all pitches that he throws as changeups. **Velo** is exactly what you think it is: the average miles per hour for each pitch type. **H Mov** is the number of inches of horizontal movement on the average pitch of that type, while **V Mov** is the number of inches of vertical movement on the average pitch of that type. (At Baseball Prospectus, we measure this over the long flight of the ball and include gravity into the V Mov number in order to give you the most realistic representation of what the pitch *actually* does.)

If you're wondering about the second number in brackets, that's the index for that velocity or movement compared to the league average. Like DRC+, a score of 100 means that the speed or movement is about the same as league average, while a higher score means that there's higher velocity or movement than the league average. Numbers below 100 indicate less velocity or movement than the league average.

Part 1: Team Analysis

Table for Two: Previewing the 2019 Washington Nationals

Sydney Bergman and Patrick Dubuque

SYDNEY BERGMAN: Let's start this as undramatically as possible: Projecting the 2019 Nationals' season feels like spitting in the face of the baseball gods. Predicting anything but crushing collapse either down the stretch or in the postseason seems like tempting fate, especially when PECOTA for the NL East pretty much came out as ¯_(ツ)_/¯, with a win differential of four wins between the fourth-ranked Atlanta team and the Nationals. So, the division is shruggie and the Marlins.

As a fan, I'm looking forward to having a tight division race, though as a potential anxiety- and ulcer-haver, I am not. You ready to do this thing, Patrick?

PATRICK DUBUQUE: A narrow first-place finish, without time to rest/reset the rotation, means a weary first round divisional playoff series. Checks out from my point of view. (Sorry.) Sure, they lost Harper, but despite that loss I found that I really like the way this Nationals team is put together.

SYDNEY: I do as well—this feels like one of the strongest teams they've fielded in a while (possibly since the glory days of 2012?), and the outfielder factory seems to be up and working. We'll talk about Dozier, but between him and Kendrick, it'll be good to have an infield without a… glaring defensive hole in it.

What part of the team can you simply not go along with PECOTA on?

SYDNEY: I went into this expecting to just disagree that PECOTA has Eaton over Rendon for WARP (3.8 vs. 3.1), which I don't agree with, in part because of I think Rendon's a better defender than what FRAA is claiming he is (-5.3! What?), and don't think Eaton is as good of one as PECOTA places him as (19.2! Again, what?)

PATRICK: Eaton's 2019 WARP is based on his 2019 FRAA, and that FRAA is so high because his 2016 score (39.7!) still has its thumb on the scale. Obviously, projection systems can't see X-rays, and when you use the old look-at-all-three-defensive-metrics trick on Rendon, FRAA is definitely the Russian judge. So I think it's fair to disagree with PECOTA on this one.

SYDNEY: If it's OK to compare Rendon's FRAA (-1.6 and -5.7 in 2017 and 8) and UZR (12.1 and 5.9 over the same years), the latter tends to overestimate his defensive capabilities when factored into fWAR, while the former seems to underestimate them. Most defensive metrics are, honestly, a step above augury in terms of their reliability and inter-site validation, and Rendon has been consistently overshadowed by certain other NL third baseman in terms of defense. So, I think his PECOTA, which has him above Eaton in terms of hitting capability, will also play out in his actual WARP. He's entering free agency after this season, but has expressed interest in remaining in Washington. If he quietly has a great, but not-quite-Gold-Glove-winning defensive season, that's going to be a payday, if we're still planning to pay free agents in the year 2020.

What player do you see collapsing in 2019?

PATRICK: OK, so you're going to have to help me on this one. Because I have to make a confession: as a citizen of the Other Coast as well as the Other League, I've never really understood Ryan Zimmerman.

Zimmerman belongs to a very select and very weird club: the players whose reputations exceed them without anyone really knowing why. I spent the last forty-eight hours asking all my friends to guess, without looking, how many All-Star games he made: the median was five. The correct answer is two. Was it because he was the only guy around in the aughts (though even then he couldn't get auto-selected)? Was it because he was a $/WAR bargain in the era where we all really idolized "bargain" players? Did we spend so long waiting for him to reach his potential that we all just kind of credited him for it when the injuries hit?

SYDNEY: How do I begin to explain Ryan Zimmerman? He is not flawless. I don't know if he has Fendi purses or a silver Lexus. One time, he tried to stop Bryce Harper from punching Hunter Strickland in the face—it was awesome.

The serious answer is that Zimmerman is neither as bad as his detractors pretend or as good as the Nationals fanbase hoped he'd be. He was the third-baseman-of-the-future and now he's the first-baseman-of-the-present. But he benefits from the 'nobody picks on him but us' mentality that any new fanbase has, and as the most veteran player of a club that once boasted a pre-Tony-Plush Nyjer Morgan, he's all we had for a long time. (Other than Ian Desmond, who the Nationals fanbase feels similarly toward.)

PATRICK: I get that. But his flawed and less lovable backup, Matt Adams, projects to be an improvement both offensively and defensively. Given how tight we've already established this pennant race is going to be, are the Nationals paying too high a price for his veteran leadership?

SYDNEY: I disagree that Matt Adams is less lovable. How can you not love someone whose nickname is *Big Mayo*? All things being equal, would Ryan Zimmerman be on the 2019 Nationals? I'm not sure—but he's projected to hit .261 and have a fairly equivalent offensive season to his mayonnaise counterpart. (And he had a mediocre 2015 and an abysmal 2016, both of which are likely weighing on his projections.) He may have a hot spring or summer, as he's done the past two years—and he may be in free agent purgatory after this season—but unless he has a season that's the literal surface of the sun in terms of hitting production, I don't see the Lerners offering him another long-term contract when they can get younger, cheaper, and better.

How did the team approach the offseason, and did they do well given their aims?

PATRICK: In an offseason where the hot stove was so cold that people burned printed articles about the economic landscape of baseball for warmth, the Nationals quietly… had a good offseason? It's amazing that signing the top pitcher in free agency to a lucrative contract in November would qualify as quiet, but November feels so long ago that Patrick Corbin may as well be a year into his deal.

For all the talk of managing contention windows and manipulating service time, Ted Lerner & Co. looked at his veteran ballclub and went and added a bunch of veterans to it. It's the simplest, least sexy roster strategy we've seen since the early 2010s Tigers, and here in March, it looks pretty effective. I don't know if it's zigging while everyone else zags, or blindly hurtling forward while everyone else zags, but the Nationals seem to have spackled together a pretty solid roster.

SYDNEY: Spending money? On a baseball team? In order to *win*? Sounds fake but OK. In all seriousness, the Lerners are sometimes penny-wise and pound-foolish—see not resigning Dusty Baker for what was, effectively, Joe Blanton money—but they haven't been as averse to signing big contracts when necessary and aren't banking on the farm system to provide everything. The team has something of an outfielder traffic jam; I don't foresee that Michael A. Taylor with be A National for much longer. But with the offseason being somewhere near 0 Kelvin, I don't see him off the team until after Spring Training when teams might actually start making moves. (Ironically, Kelvin Herrera has signed with the White Sox.)

That said, in looking at the Nats holistically, the team could probably probably use more lefty relievers. Sure, but that's a) true of every team and b) my lingering resentment of allowing Óliver Pérez to get picked up by Cleveland, only to have a career-best season. The Nats currently have only Sammy 'Cada Dia o Nada Dia' Solis, Sean Doolittle, and Matt Grace. But the dearth of bullpen lefties is something we (the Nationals fanbase) has mentioned every offseason for a while, so I feel that this is also a problem we've learned to live with.

PATRICK: Obviously, it's going to be weird to see this team in action without Bryce Harper on it, but at least the team took their Harper money and used it to make other bets. But what I find so interesting about the roster is the second-tier signings they made, spackling in low-ceiling, medium-floor veterans like Brian Dozier, Anibal Sanchez and Jeremy Hellickson to hold down weak spots on the roster. They're the kind of deals most fans hate, because fans want players to hang their dreams on, and the only dream Hellickson supplies is one of those

Washington Nationals 2019

"dream you went to work and then wake up and realize you have to get ready to go to work" ones. (Sydney: He was the 2011 ROY so at the very least is a dream where you signed up for a class and then never attended, and are now failing.)

There's a sort of confidence to these kinds of moves I find appealing: The Nationals are saying, in essence, the rest of our team is good enough that we don't need upside at the periphery. Do you agree with that philosophy? Or are you going to find yourself dreading the days when the back of the rotation shows up, and Joe Ross is out there still not figuring it out?

SYDNEY: I think Baby Joe is going to be a good third or fourth starter—the team has a good history of rehabbing pitchers from TJ (*cough* Stras shutdown *cough*). He was rocky in 2017 but hasn't pitched more than 100 innings since 2016, so we're operating on a relatively low sample size for a pitcher who's only 25.

I also think that the move of getting two solid, good-hitting catchers rather than one superstar like Realmuto isn't a bad one. Either would have been an upgrade from Wieters and at this point, sorting catchers with more than 100 games in 2018 by OPS+ and just grabbing the two who were available (including a fan-favorite from a few years ago) looks fairly genius, considering how little other teams have done in the off-season.

PATRICK: Do we want to talk about Harper?

SYDNEY: *wearing a sackcloth and ashes* What do you mean? I'm fine.

But for real, Bryce Harper told us he was leaving, and then he left. He also told us he was going to get paid—hell, I even said that he should go and get paid, because baseball isn't played for sentiment but for money, no matter what billionaire owners claim—and then he went and got paid. I can't be mad at that, even if it means we'll see him all the freaking time. To put it another way, this isn't just a break-up, but one where you gotta see your ex at a lot of parties, the ex who's now in a committed long-term relationship with someone that most analysts agree are (almost) as good-looking as you are, if by 'good-looking' I mean 'expected number of wins predicted by PECOTA.'

And in light of the fact that Bryce has spent the off-season playing will-they-or-won't-they with signing, all of the moves we've talked about before Harper announced he was giving the Phillies the rose, Bachelor-style, look both smart and safe. The Nationals don't really need to dream audaciously at this point—just field a good team based on the straightforward strategy of 'a few great players, some more good ones, and also Wilmer Difo, who is a delight.' The rest is hoping that the season plays out without significant injury or derailment (TFU TFU TFU), even with Harp playing against us and not with for us.

What's your prediction for this team?

PATRICK: Obviously, the NL East is going to be a gauntlet. But some team, by rule, has to win it, and I feel like the Nationals are the surest bet of any, thanks to their well-rounded roster, to survive all the way to the end. I do think they'll need one more starter–I spent a week researching Anibal Sanchez last fall, trying to figure out how he'd turned it around, and there is just no good explanation beyond "suddenly stopped missing the outside corner"–but half the league could use a better fourth starter. So I'm going to say 90 wins, and, as hot as the takes come, an actual NLCS appearance.

SYDNEY: Patrick, why are we tempting fate? I'm going to say a tie for 87 wins and a 1-game 'play-off' to get into the postseason similar to what happened in the NL Central and West in 2018, culminating in the team losing in spectacular but predictable fashion to the Phillies.

PATRICK: Wow, that's dark. Even for me.

Performance Graphs

2018 Hit List Ranking

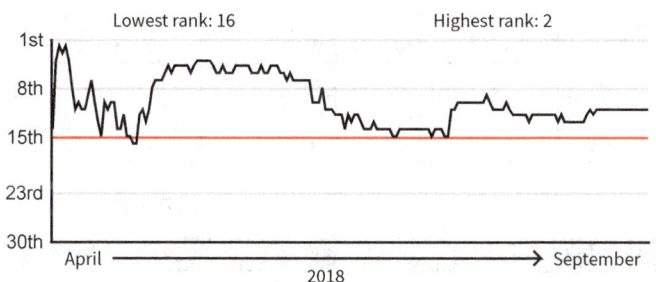

Committed Payroll (in millions)

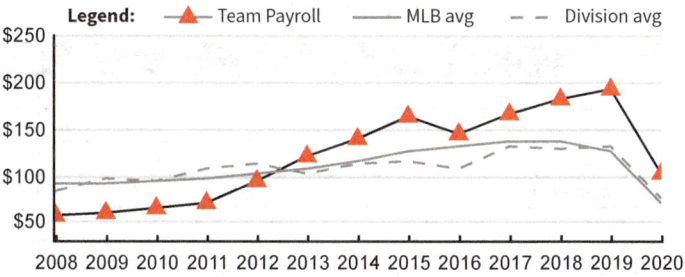

Farm System Ranking

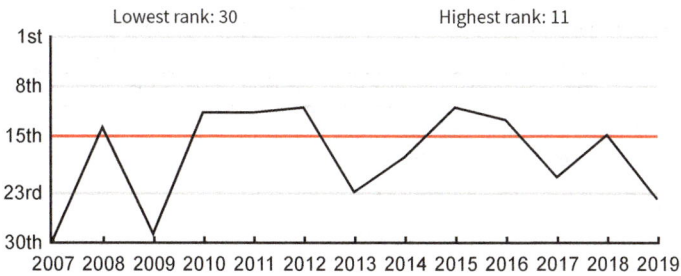

2018 Team Performance

ACTUAL STANDINGS

Team	W	L	Pct
ATL	90	72	.555
WAS	**82**	**80**	**.506**
PHI	80	82	.493
NYN	77	85	.475
MIA	63	98	.391

THIRD-ORDER STANDINGS

Team	W	L	Pct
ATL	94	68	.580
WAS	**91**	**71**	**.561**
NYN	79	83	.487
PHI	79	83	.487
MIA	63	98	.391

TOP HITTERS

Player	WARP
Trea Turner	5
Anthony Rendon	4.4
Juan Soto	3

TOP PITCHERS

Player	WARP
Max Scherzer	7.7
Stephen Strasburg	3.5
Austin Adams	2

VITAL STATISTICS

Statistic Name	Value	Rank
Pythagenpat	.557	10th
Runs Scored per Game	4.76	8th
Runs Allowed per Game	4.21	12th
Deserved Runs Created Plus	97	14th
Deserved Run Average	4.31	14th
Fielding Independent Pitching	4.11	19th
Defensive Efficiency Rating	.713	8th
Batter Age	27.3	8th
Pitcher Age	30.2	29th
Salary	$179.8M	5th
Marginal $ per Marginal Win	$5.0M	8th
Disabled List Days	$1,396.0M	24th
$ on DL	18%	17th

2019 Team Projections

PROJECTED STANDINGS

Team	W	L	Pct	+/-
WAS	89	73	.549	+7
NYN	87	75	.537	+10
ATL	85	77	.524	-5
PHI	85	77	.524	+5
MIA	68	94	.419	+5

TOP PROJECTED HITTERS

Player	WARP
Trea Turner	4.4
Adam Eaton	4.0
Juan Soto	3.7

TOP PROJECTED PITCHERS

Player	WARP
Max Scherzer	4.0
Patrick Corbin	3.3
Stephen Strasburg	3.1

FARM SYSTEM REPORT

Top Prospect	Number of Top 101 Prospects
Victor Robles, #5	3

KEY DEDUCTIONS

Player	WARP
Bryce Harper	3.6
Tanner Roark	0.8
Mark Reynolds	0.3

KEY ADDITIONS

Player	WARP
Patrick Corbin	3.3
Brian Dozier	2.5
Kurt Suzuki	1.2
Anibal Sanchez	1.1
Yan Gomes	1.0
Kyle Barraclough	0.4

Team Personnel

General Manager
Mike Rizzo

Assistant General Manager
Doug Harris

Assistant General Manager
Kris Kline

Manager
Dave Martinez

Nationals Park Stats

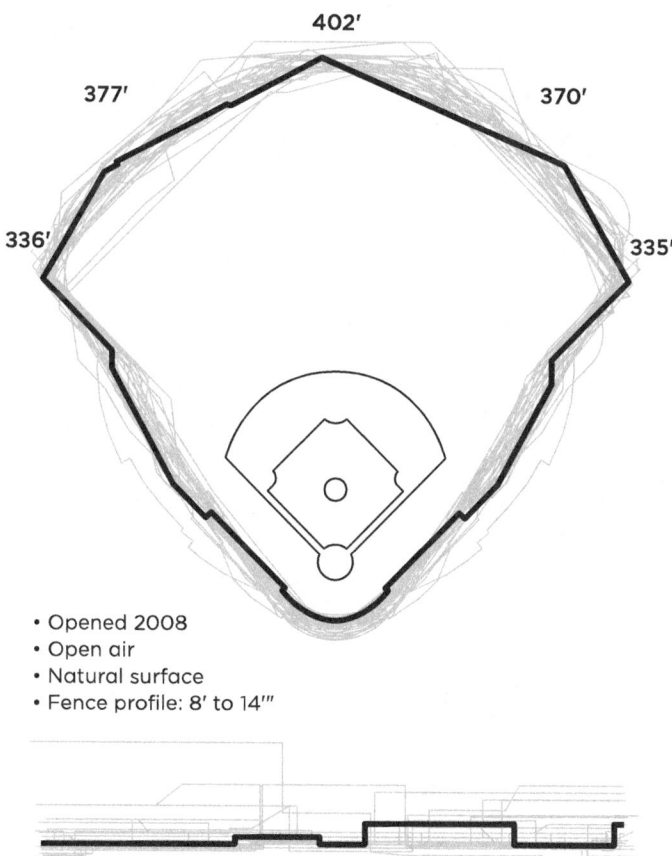

- Opened 2008
- Open air
- Natural surface
- Fence profile: 8' to 14'"

Three-Year Park Factors

Runs	Runs/RH	Runs/LH	HR/RH	HR/LH
103	104	100	107	99

Nationals Team Analysis

An odd affliction exists in baseball, borne of success and timing, and that is that once your team is possessed of a baseball god, people expect you to do something with him. Not tiny somethings; not squeaking-by things. But big things, World Series things, baseball history things. Baseball gods are not little mice; baseball gods are mammoth, titan. Baseball gods alter the course of a franchise, should a franchise let them.

The Los Angeles Angels are familiar with this condition; it itches under the skin when you watch Mike Trout roam center field only to remember his relative absence from October, exiled as he has mostly been from the pantheon we hold most dear. The Washington Nationals have done considerably better by their time with Bryce Harper, though the futility that has ultimately marked those years inspires its own bit of scratching. It has become an era defined as much by how far the franchise didn't go as how far it did. You can understand why. Harper is, as he has been since before he could drive, resplendent. He exudes the bright, insistent bravado of his hometown, though unlike Las Vegas, and its faux-New York and Paris, the "ancient" "Rome" of Caesars, and leagues of concert fondant masking a sea of plastic, Harper has weight and substance, to the tune of 30.5 WARP. He was moved off catcher upon drafting; how many gods pass their time in a crouch, their faces obscured? He's won Rookie of the Year and MVP honors, and been the first-overall pick and a six-time All-Star. The god glistens.

And now the god is leaving. To call his time in Washington a waste is to misunderstand one of the Greeks' (and baseball's) other great conceits: tragedy. His dearth of rings aside, Bryce Harper has never experienced a losing season. He has glimpsed October. But one can't exactly call his tenure a triumph either. The Nationals have lost. Not completely or always right away, but ultimately and decisively. How they've lost with a god in tow has varied. Let us review the ways.

2012 and 2013: The Hubris of Faith

It gets lost in the talk of heroes and thunder, but some gods turn out to be fools. They concern themselves overly with the machinations of farmers or sailors; they covet human lovers. They disappoint, not immune from being ridiculous. To roster a god is insufficient to guarantee triumph; you have to learn what sort he is. Bryce Harper wasn't sure to be a destroyer of worlds. He could have been an imposing but hapless jester; baseball has a way of exposing those.

Washington Nationals 2019

But Harper's rookie campaign revealed him to be exactly what Washington expected: a champion. He shimmered, just 19 years old and soaring, as he worked his way to 5.2 WARP and Rookie of the Year honors. He was the youngest player to hit a home run in the majors since Adrian Beltre; the first teenager to steal home since 1964. A down July and August were but the trials gods go through to prove their mettle; the concern that such struggles suggested something more permanent would prove to be a clown question, bro. He was a hero arrived.

Of course, his was not the only journey 2012 witnessed. On September 12 of that year, Stephen Strasburg threw his final start of the season; he would not return for the playoffs, made unavailable by fretting over UCLs and the possibility of longer absences. He would watch as the Cardinals rallied for four runs in Game 5 of the NLDS, but just watch. 2013 would prove devastating; the Nationals missed the playoffs entirely. The Strasburg decision loomed large. It could be called hubris, or an overabundance of caution; perhaps it was both those things. But it was also an act of faith, an assumption on the part of General Manager Mike Rizzo that this was but the start of a long run of postseasons and parades. That there was more time. Wars among gods and monsters unfurl over millennia, after all, and the divine don't age like the rest of us.

2014: Even-Year Bullshit

Even Zeus doesn't always win. All gods have their machinations, their trials and favorites, their battles to be won and lost, and they are themselves subject to forces and castings. The 2014 Nationals won 96 games. They took the NL East by 17. Harper missed 62 games after tearing a ligament in his thumb. His June 28, 2014 Double-A rehab start, during which he slugged three home runs, was the stuff of legend. But so was Even-Year Bullshit. The Nationals lost the NLDS to the Giants, three games to one. San Francisco would go on to win its second World Series in three years.

2015: Meddlesome Mortals

The gods get a bad rap for meddling in the affairs of men, but plucky mortals have also been known to court their own disaster. When starting a fight against one of Zeus' ilk, it's best to be sure you can win; the truly savvy among the human set align themselves with the sublime, looking to play a minor role in a hero's story, rather than lead the charge themselves. But there are always dopes. In 2015, Jonathan Papelbon was but a man, all puffery and pugnacity. Harper, coming off a 2014 marred by injuries, was about to become the youngest unanimous MVP winner in baseball history. He was about to post 9.7 WARP. He was about to collide with Papelbon's pluck. Literally. On September 27, the god and the man tilted at each other in the Nationals dugout after Harper loafed to first a bit slower than Papelbon would have liked and Harper took offense at

Papelbon's umbrage. During the skirmish, Papelbon put his hands to Harper's throat, and shoved him. He would end the season suspended, unable to hide that he was a dope, misaligned against his true foes.

It isn't what undid Washington's 2015; injuries and underperformance elsewhere on the roster, and an opaque but pronounced ennui, seem to have done that. October baseball would not be the team's only casualty. Matt Williams and his coaching staff were left in the season's depths. Drew Storen's hand broke under the force of his own disappointment. But the fight carried with it the flavor of 2015's failure: Bryce was ready to ascend, buoyed by a heavenly host, and Max Scherzer's two no-hitters, while the rest of his squad remained earthbound, all pluck and undone plans.

2016: Other Gods Make Their Presence Felt

Of course, baseball isn't a monotheistic religion. Its battles are witness to all sorts of lesser deities and otherworldly competitors, and it isn't governed by fairness. With your season on the line, with your hopes and dreams and a golden fleece in peril, you'd prefer a hero equal to the task, able to match up against the other team's immortals, and throw some rocks at them. But that isn't always what you get. Sometimes, despite six innings of one run ball in Game 5 of the NLDS from Max Scherzer, himself the stuff of Olympus, you find yourself undone by Marc Rzepczynski, Blake Treinen, and Sammy Solis. Sometimes a rally begun against Grant Dayton is squashed when Kenley Jansen enters in the seventh. Sometimes, you're Bryce Harper, standing on second base after having walked in the ninth, helpless to do anything but look on as Clayton Kershaw enters the arena, tense and deadly, and ready to feast. Sometimes, all your team can offer is a sacrifice. You, Bryce, stand there, watching as Wilmer Difo is swallowed up, a bit of fuel to one of your divine fellows righting his own postseason tale.

The worst part of being a baseball god must come in realizing the mortality of others.

2017: Mischief Reigns

Fans tend to ascribe their own particular rooting interests to the so-called Baseball Gods. Not the gods who descend from the ethereal plain to hurl lightning or shatter the sky with the *thwack!* of their bats, all flowing hair and fist pumps and glory, but the middle managers. The keepers of scores and hamstrings and trophies. Perhaps that sort is possessed of fandom; maybe some divine Janus or Glen whoops in delight when his favorite team records the final out of their World Series win. But it seems just as likely that his motivations are smaller, stranger, the result of grudges and petty nonsense among his kind that mere mortals can scarce understand.

To wit, Game 5 of the 2017 NLDS had all the hallmarks of some magical trickster who wasn't so much interested in another Cubs parade as he was in a bit of mischief at the Nationals' expense. Matt Wieters was hit in the mask by the backswing of a dropped, swinging third strike; it ought to have nullified a passed ball and a throwing error but went uncalled. A batter later, Tommy La Stella reached on catcher's interference. Scherzer, on in relief, hit Jon Jay to drive in a run. Later, with two on and two out in the eighth, it was determined that Willson Contreras had picked Jose Lobaton off at first after a Cubs' challenge overturned the call on the field. Down a run in the ninth, Harper struck out swinging against Wade Davis to end Washington's season, a god felled by one of his number, just not one at the park. It could have gone differently; Harper might have forced extras, where perhaps a triumph loomed. But he didn't. Not because the gods are Cubs fans, but because some sprite named Glen preferred a bit of funny business. Even 97 wins can't save you (or Dusty Baker) from that.

2018: The Twilight of a Time

2018 never did seem like it was going to go quite right. Despite being strongly favored to win their division, the Nationals once again stumbled under their own weight. Once again, there were hints of clubhouse discord, this time under new manager Dave Martinez. Once again there were injuries. And Harper, a season away from free agency, endured an odd and uncomfortable thing for a god; he had his record examined, his seasons measured, his defense weighed, the ticks above average accounted for. It is impossible to deny what Harper is capable of being, but much of 2018 was spent contemplating what he had been. Sometimes injured; often mercurial. Prone to fit and fuss when displeased. Perhaps a different sort of god when stripped of his MVP season and the power it granted him. 2018 was supposed to be a rush of triumph, a last ride up that dusty mountain; a World Series. It was supposed to be a passing of a time into its twilight, with one star left shining. Only that star wasn't Harper. All that reflecting back naturally shifted to looking forward, and we begin to see that the Nationals story isn't ending. A new god emerges, born from the head of scouts and player development personnel and his own muster. Bryce will seek out new lands, but Juan Soto could assume his mantle. Max Scherzer and Stephen Strasburg will be there, and Patrick Corbin will join their number; ownership may have balked at Harper's weight in gold, but they have used some treasure. Adam Eaton should be healthy. Victor Robles looms. They might finally sing songs of Anthony Rendon. Trea Turner is just 25. It seems impossible that the bullpen could be as bad again.

The Nationals aren't a story that ends so much as a crew about to set sail into the second part of their epic. Odysseus is done with all that business in Troy; it's time to set out for Ithaca, or at least 2019. There will be new monsters and champions, perils and triumphs, and for the first time since Harper was drafted in 2010, Washington will face them without their strange affliction. You might be expected to do something when possessed of a baseball god, but now, a god departs. Turn the page. ∎

—Meg Rowley is the Managing Editor of FanGraphs.

Part 2: Player Analysis

Matt Adams 1B

Born: 08/31/88   Age: 30   Bats: L   Throws: R
Height: 6'3"   Weight: 245   Origin: Round 23, 2009 Draft (#699 overall)

YEAR	TEAM	LVL	AGE	PA	R	2B	3B	HR	RBI	BB	K	SB	CS	AVG/OBP/SLG
2016	SLN	MLB	27	327	37	18	0	16	54	25	81	0	1	.249/.309/.471
2017	SLN	MLB	28	53	4	2	0	1	7	4	17	0	0	.292/.340/.396
2017	ATL	MLB	28	314	42	20	1	19	58	19	71	0	0	.271/.315/.543
2018	WAS	MLB	29	277	37	9	0	18	48	24	55	0	0	.257/.332/.510
2018	SLN	MLB	29	60	5	1	0	3	9	3	18	0	0	.158/.200/.333
2019	WAS	MLB	30	249	30	12	1	11	35	20	57	0	0	.258/.325/.467

Breakout: 1%   Improve: 31%   Collapse: 23%   Attrition: 14%   MLB: 92%
Comparables: Mitch Moreland, Ben Broussard, Hal Breeden

For another half a season, Adams showed that tantalizing potential to bloom as a slugging first baseman. He was, in fact, more convincing than ever. He cut his strikeout rate down, boosted his walk rate, and still accessed every bit of his over-the-fence power (though he was spraying the ball and lining it to the gaps less often, as nearly every player does in their late 20s). It was technically a broken finger that derailed him, sidelining him around the All-Star break and apparently sapping all those gains he'd made even when he returned. In truth, though, this seems to be Adams's modest fate. He keeps demonstrating real improvement and moving toward a full season of terrific run production, but he also keeps being beaten back—and beaten in the zone, by good fastballs.

YEAR	TEAM	LVL	AGE	PA	DRC+	VORP	BABIP	BRR	FRAA	WARP
2016	SLN	MLB	27	327	103	8.5	.286	-2.4	1B(86): 9.3	1.3
2017	SLN	MLB	28	53	106	1.8	.419	-0.1	LF(6): -0.3, 1B(3): 0.1	0.2
2017	ATL	MLB	28	314	109	14.0	.294	-0.6	1B(59): -3.3, LF(13): 0.5	0.6
2018	WAS	MLB	29	277	110	10.5	.261	-2.3	1B(48): 0.3, LF(15): 0.7	0.7
2018	SLN	MLB	29	60	115	-3.2	.167	0.0	1B(15): -0.5	0.2
2019	WAS	MLB	30	249	112	8.8	.296	-0.5	1B 2	1.1

Matt Adams, continued

Batted Ball Distribution

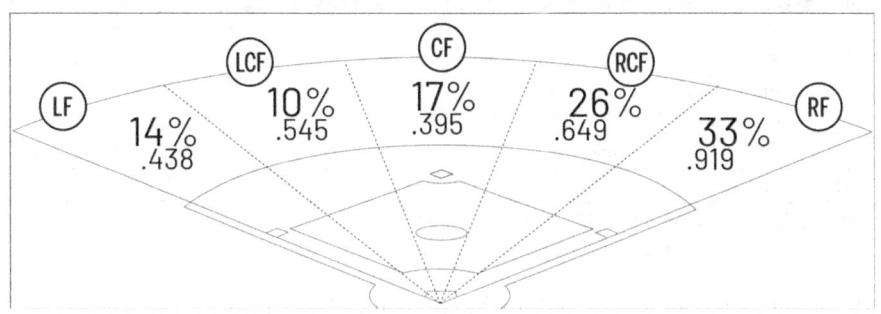

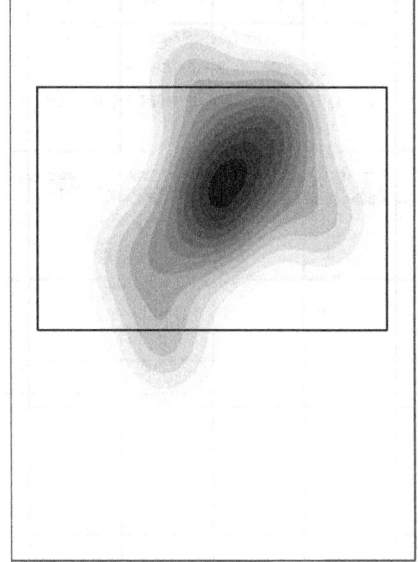

Strike Zone vs LHP

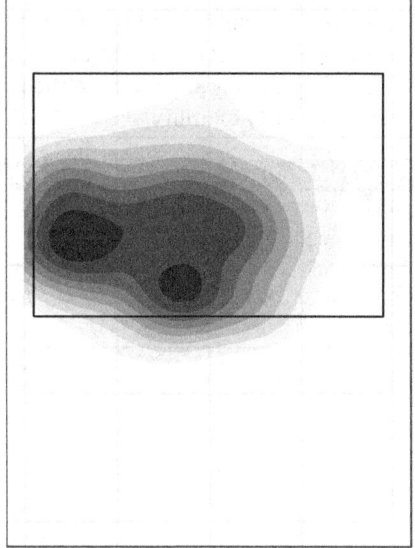

Strike Zone vs RHP

Wilmer Difo 2B
Born: 04/02/92   Age: 27   Bats: B   Throws: R
Height: 5'11"   Weight: 200   Origin: International Free Agent, 2010

YEAR	TEAM	LVL	AGE	PA	R	2B	3B	HR	RBI	BB	K	SB	CS	AVG/OBP/SLG
2016	HAR	AA	24	451	59	15	3	6	41	34	59	28	11	.259/.318/.354
2016	WAS	MLB	24	66	14	3	0	1	7	8	12	3	0	.276/.364/.379
2017	SYR	AAA	25	45	5	2	0	0	1	5	6	0	0	.175/.267/.225
2017	WAS	MLB	25	365	47	10	4	5	21	24	74	10	1	.271/.319/.370
2018	WAS	MLB	26	456	55	14	7	7	42	39	82	10	3	.230/.298/.350
2019	WAS	MLB	27	303	35	12	3	6	29	26	59	9	2	.247/.316/.380

Breakout: 13%   Improve: 48%   Collapse: 13%   Attrition: 27%   MLB: 88%
Comparables: Tyler Saladino, Brandon Phillips, Russ Adams

The 1990s called asking about Difo, but hung up when they heard he doesn't even steal that many bases. It's not his fault that the Nationals bestowed even more plate appearances upon his feeble bat in 2018, but he ended up as one of the roster holes that cut down a should-have-been-a-contender team. In Difo's defense, he drew a few more walks while striking out a little less than in 2017, and he wasn't really any worse than he's ever been in the big leagues. Still, a .250/.310/.358 career line won't pass muster as a starter in any era, although Difo's ability to play anywhere in the infield and occasionally even in the outfield gives him plenty of utility.

YEAR	TEAM	LVL	AGE	PA	DRC+	VORP	BABIP	BRR	FRAA	WARP
2016	HAR	AA	24	451	88	13.9	.288	-0.1	SS(103): -2.4	0.5
2016	WAS	MLB	24	66	84	3.1	.333	1.0	2B(9): 0.2, SS(5): 0.2	0.3
2017	SYR	AAA	25	45	73	-1.8	.206	-0.1	SS(9): -1.4, CF(2): -0.3	-0.2
2017	WAS	MLB	25	365	78	9.0	.332	2.4	SS(57): 7.1, 2B(25): -0.7	1.3
2018	WAS	MLB	26	456	79	0.5	.269	-1.5	2B(112): 4.7, 3B(20): -0.8	0.6
2019	WAS	MLB	27	303	86	5.6	.293	1.1	SS 1, 3B -1	0.7

Wilmer Difo, continued

Batted Ball Distribution

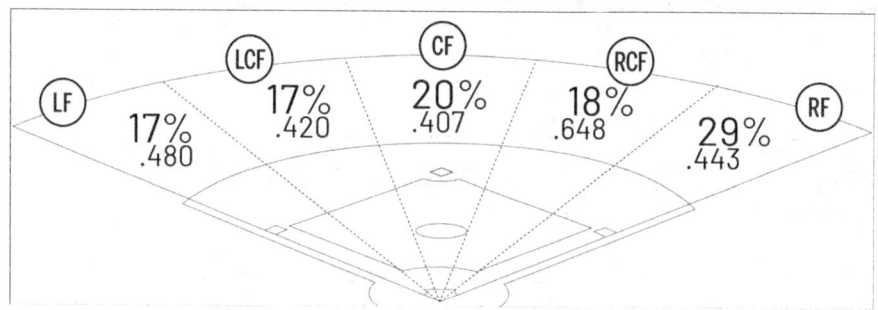

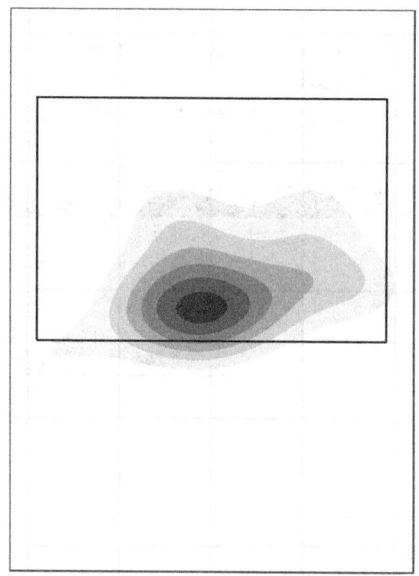

Strike Zone vs LHP

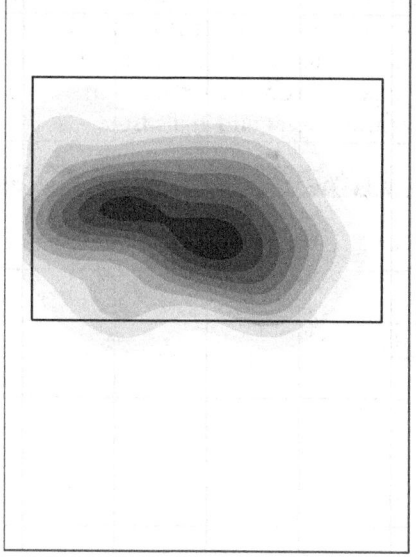

Strike Zone vs RHP

Brian Dozier 2B

Born: 05/15/87 Age: 32 Bats: R Throws: R
Height: 5'11" Weight: 200 Origin: Round 8, 2009 Draft (#252 overall)

YEAR	TEAM	LVL	AGE	PA	R	2B	3B	HR	RBI	BB	K	SB	CS	AVG/OBP/SLG
2016	MIN	MLB	29	691	104	35	5	42	99	61	138	18	2	.268/.340/.546
2017	MIN	MLB	30	705	106	30	4	34	93	78	141	16	7	.271/.359/.498
2018	MIN	MLB	31	462	65	21	2	16	52	46	96	8	3	.227/.307/.405
2018	LAN	MLB	31	170	16	9	0	5	20	24	33	4	0	.182/.300/.350
2019	WAS	MLB	32	482	63	23	2	19	63	51	97	11	3	.254/.339/.453

Breakout: 1% Improve: 35% Collapse: 19% Attrition: 10% MLB: 100%
Comparables: Rickie Weeks, Mark Ellis, Aaron Hill

After flirting with the Dodgers for a couple years over Dozier's services, Minnesota finally succumbed to L.A.'s charm and sent the former All Star west in a July deal. The result was the biggest Minnesota-to-Hollywood disappointment since Fargo got passed over for Best Picture in 1996. A lingering knee injury drove Dozier to develop some bad habits at the plate, subsequently sapping the slugger's power and leading to his lowest DRC+ since his rookie year. While second basemen on the wrong side of 30 typically age like guacamole in the heat, Dozier has never spent a day on the disabled list and still smacked 21 dingers in a down season, so there's reason to believe his first free-agent contract won't end in disaster.

YEAR	TEAM	LVL	AGE	PA	DRC+	VORP	BABIP	BRR	FRAA	WARP
2016	MIN	MLB	29	691	128	41.4	.280	1.1	2B(151): -2.2	4.3
2017	MIN	MLB	30	705	123	37.0	.300	2.2	2B(152): 9.7	5.4
2018	MIN	MLB	31	462	97	11.6	.256	1.6	2B(103): 1.9	1.6
2018	LAN	MLB	31	170	97	-1.6	.196	-1.6	2B(45): 0.1	0.3
2019	WAS	MLB	32	482	112	25.3	.287	0.6	2B 0	2.5

Brian Dozier, continued

Batted Ball Distribution

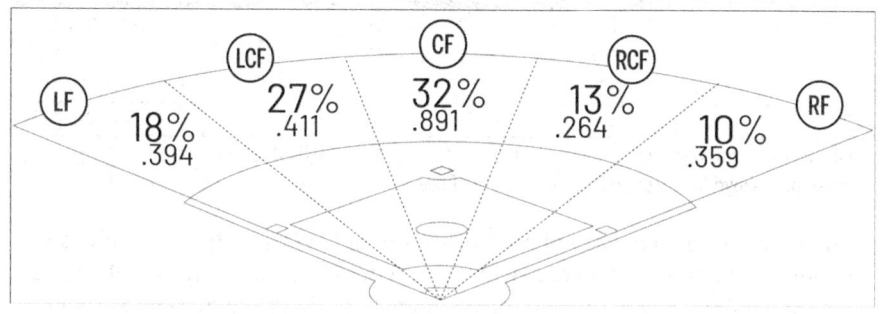

Strike Zone vs LHP

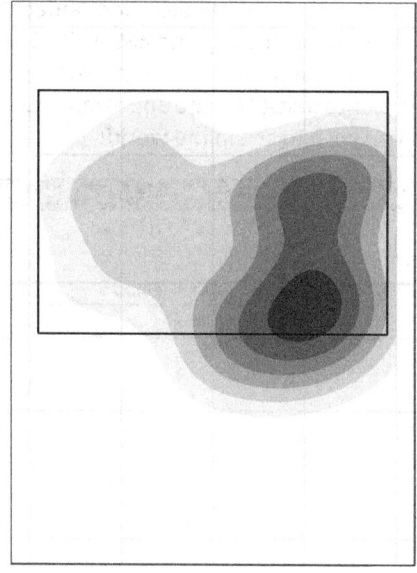

Strike Zone vs RHP

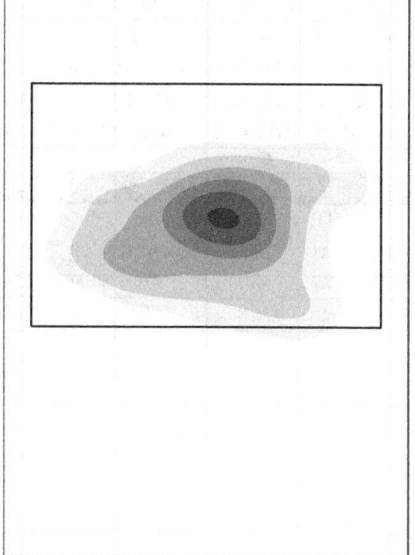

Washington Nationals 2019

Adam Eaton   RF
Born: 12/06/88   Age: 30   Bats: L   Throws: L
Height: 5'9"   Weight: 176   Origin: Round 19, 2010 Draft (#571 overall)

YEAR	TEAM	LVL	AGE	PA	R	2B	3B	HR	RBI	BB	K	SB	CS	AVG/OBP/SLG
2016	CHA	MLB	27	706	91	29	9	14	59	63	115	14	5	.284/.362/.428
2017	WAS	MLB	28	107	24	7	1	2	13	14	18	3	1	.297/.393/.462
2018	WAS	MLB	29	370	55	18	1	5	33	38	64	9	1	.301/.394/.411
2019	WAS	MLB	30	558	73	25	3	11	52	53	102	12	3	.271/.354/.402

Breakout: 1%   Improve: 46%   Collapse: 14%   Attrition: 4%   MLB: 99%
Comparables: Floyd Robinson, Harvey Kuenn, Pete Rose

Comrades: I write on the eve of our third summer in Washington to thank you for your efforts thus far, and to ask that you redouble your commitment against the tyranny of the Evil Eaton. We the ligaments, tendons and muscles serving under inhumane conditions imposed upon us by Eaton and his co-conspirators this year welcomed bones to our coalition — and seek to enlist further support for our cause in the coming days from bursa and fascia. Together, we will unite. If you ever doubt the power of your sacrifice, remember that Eaton demanded and received 706 grueling plate appearances from us in 2016, and 689 in 2015 — topping 10.0 WARP over two years on the back of our labor. Since organizing on the voyage to D.C., we have held our tormentor to just 477 plate appearances. Take pride, and in conclusion: Be the pain you wish to see in the world!

YEAR	TEAM	LVL	AGE	PA	DRC+	VORP	BABIP	BRR	FRAA	WARP
2016	CHA	MLB	27	706	108	32.9	.329	5.9	RF(121): 33.4, CF(48): 6.3	7.2
2017	WAS	MLB	28	107	100	9.5	.347	0.3	CF(20): -3.3, LF(5): 0.4	0.1
2018	WAS	MLB	29	370	106	20.4	.364	0.4	RF(67): 5.7, LF(10): -0.5	1.7
2019	WAS	MLB	30	558	104	21.3	.318	0.6	RF 21	4.0

Adam Eaton, continued

Batted Ball Distribution

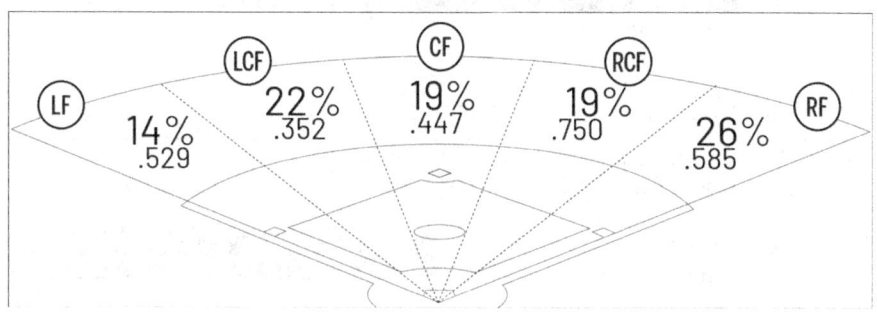

| **Strike Zone vs LHP** | **Strike Zone vs RHP** |

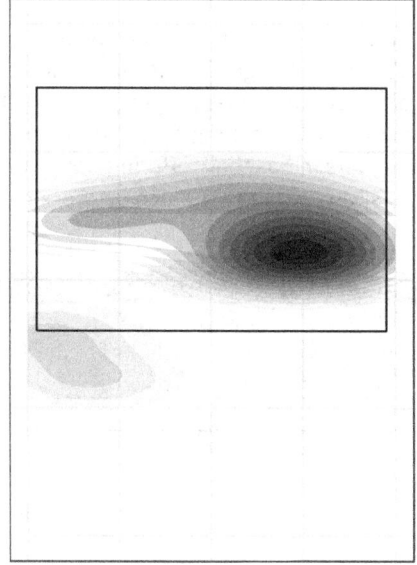 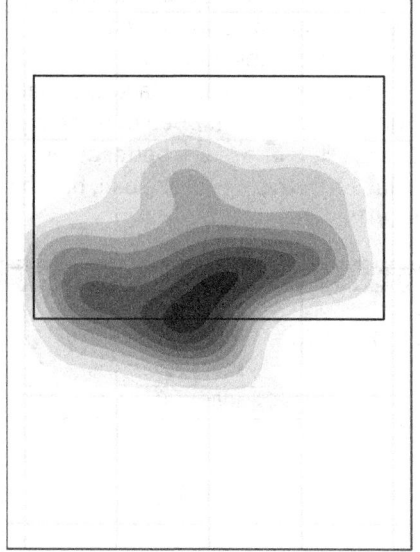

Yan Gomes C

Born: 07/19/87   Age: 31   Bats: R   Throws: R
Height: 6'2"   Weight: 215   Origin: Round 10, 2009 Draft (#310 overall)

YEAR	TEAM	LVL	AGE	PA	R	2B	3B	HR	RBI	BB	K	SB	CS	AVG/OBP/SLG
2016	CLE	MLB	28	264	22	11	1	9	34	9	69	0	0	.167/.201/.327
2017	CLE	MLB	29	383	43	15	0	14	56	31	99	0	0	.232/.309/.399
2018	CLE	MLB	30	435	52	26	0	16	48	21	119	0	0	.266/.313/.449
2019	WAS	MLB	31	318	35	15	1	10	37	22	80	0	0	.239/.302/.401

Breakout: 4%   Improve: 32%   Collapse: 30%   Attrition: 26%   MLB: 95%
Comparables: Welington Castillo, Nick Hundley, Matt Nokes

For the second straight season, the Indians enjoyed a (mostly) full season of a (mostly) healthy and (mostly) productive Gomes, which was something of a coup when you consider his struggles in both departments during the two preceding

YEAR	TEAM	P. COUNT	FRM RUNS	BLK RUNS	THRW RUNS	TOT RUNS
2016	CLE	9256	-3.2	-0.3	0.2	-3.0
2017	CLE	13358	4.2	0.5	2.3	7.6
2018	CLE	15103	7.5	1.7	0.0	9.6
2019	WAS	10304	2.5	0.4	0.5	3.4

years. That Gomes was able to catch more than 800 innings, provide above-average receiving numbers and hit around league average ain't nothing — it made him an All-Star, in fact. Cleveland's offseason payroll-shedding began with Gomes, who was shipped to Washington to tag-team catching duties with Kurt Suzuki. He's one of the better all-around catchers in baseball, offering positive value on both sides of the ball, but the time-share will likely reduce his workload in 2019.

YEAR	TEAM	LVL	AGE	PA	DRC+	VORP	BABIP	BRR	FRAA	WARP
2016	CLE	MLB	28	264	63	-7.4	.189	2.3	C(73): -4.6	-0.1
2017	CLE	MLB	29	383	92	13.2	.283	1.7	C(103): 6.8	2.4
2018	CLE	MLB	30	435	103	23.1	.336	-1.1	C(111): 9.1	3.1
2019	WAS	MLB	31	318	90	11.6	.291	-0.6	C 1	1.0

Yan Gomes, continued

Batted Ball Distribution

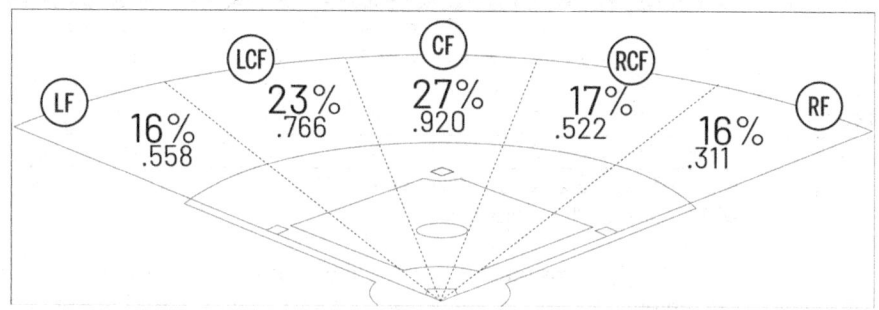

Strike Zone vs LHP

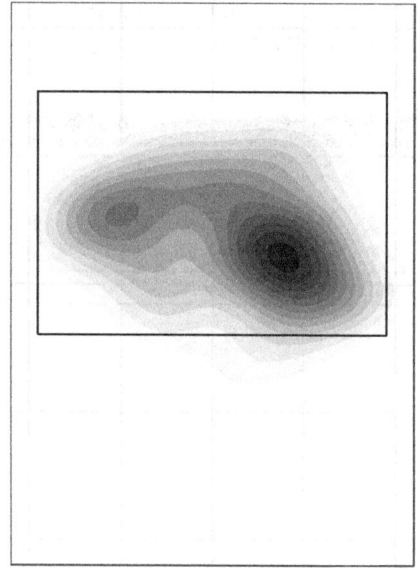

Strike Zone vs RHP

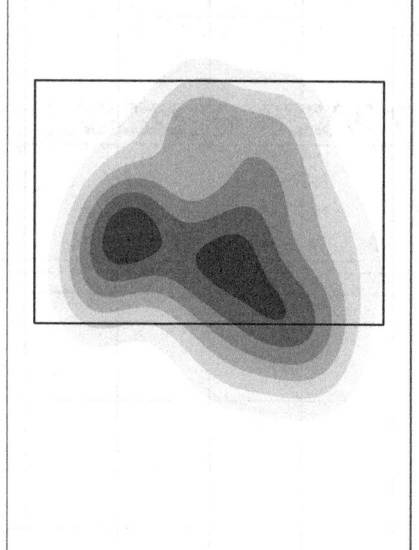

Howie Kendrick 2B

Born: 07/12/83 Age: 35 Bats: R Throws: R
Height: 5'11" Weight: 220 Origin: Round 10, 2002 Draft (#294 overall)

YEAR	TEAM	LVL	AGE	PA	R	2B	3B	HR	RBI	BB	K	SB	CS	AVG/OBP/SLG
2016	LAN	MLB	32	543	65	26	2	8	40	50	96	10	2	.255/.326/.366
2017	PHI	MLB	33	156	16	8	1	2	16	11	30	8	3	.340/.397/.454
2017	WAS	MLB	33	178	24	8	2	7	25	11	38	4	2	.293/.343/.494
2018	WAS	MLB	34	160	17	14	0	4	12	5	29	1	1	.303/.331/.474
2019	WAS	MLB	35	117	13	5	1	3	13	9	23	2	1	.264/.325/.415

Breakout: 0% Improve: 15% Collapse: 23% Attrition: 9% MLB: 79%
Comparables: Mark Ellis, Ronnie Belliard, Orlando Hudson

When the sun eventually burns out, Kendrick will presumably be hitting .290, sitting on the disabled list, or both. Come April, he'll be 35 and returning from an Achilles tendon injury, but the Nationals have him under contract for an exceedingly reasonable $4 million. As long as he can stand in the box, he's a decent bet to put the bat on the ball in just the right way to spray a line drive over the infield (you don't log a .340 BABIP over a 13-year career by accident). In other words, he's exactly the type of professional hitter who will never go out of style.

YEAR	TEAM	LVL	AGE	PA	DRC+	VORP	BABIP	BRR	FRAA	WARP
2016	LAN	MLB	32	543	87	14.6	.301	4.9	LF(94): -0.7, 2B(32): 0.5	1.0
2017	PHI	MLB	33	156	108	10.8	.418	-0.7	LF(24): -0.4, 2B(10): 0.6	0.5
2017	WAS	MLB	33	178	106	10.3	.342	0.6	LF(38): -3.0, 2B(5): -0.2	0.3
2018	WAS	MLB	34	160	94	3.8	.350	-3.1	2B(33): -2.7, LF(6): -0.1	-0.2
2019	WAS	MLB	35	117	88	2.1	.308	0.0	2B 0, 1B 0	0.1

Howie Kendrick, continued

Batted Ball Distribution

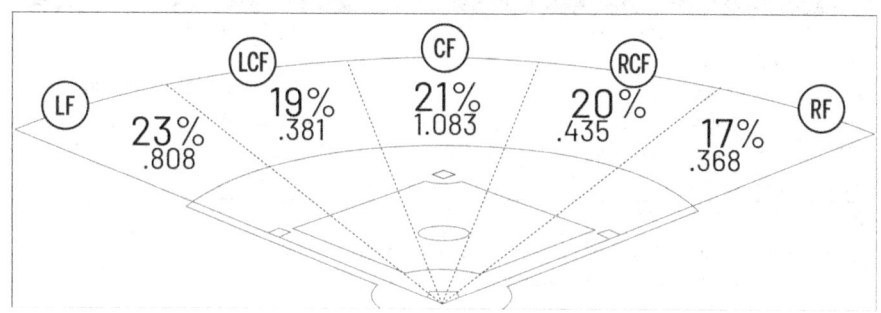

Strike Zone vs LHP **Strike Zone vs RHP**

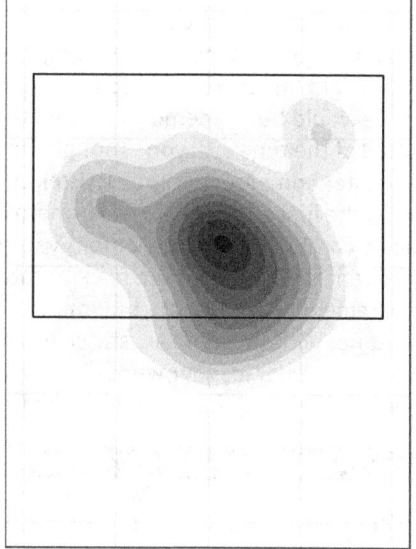

Spencer Kieboom C

Born: 03/16/91 Age: 28 Bats: R Throws: R
Height: 6'0" Weight: 210 Origin: Round 5, 2012 Draft (#174 overall)

YEAR	TEAM	LVL	AGE	PA	R	2B	3B	HR	RBI	BB	K	SB	CS	AVG/OBP/SLG
2016	HAR	AA	25	359	27	11	0	5	31	43	61	0	0	.230/.324/.314
2016	WAS	MLB	25	1	1	0	0	0	0	1	0	0	0	
2017	HAR	AA	26	70	6	5	0	2	6	10	13	0	0	.183/.300/.367
2017	SYR	AAA	26	176	17	9	0	3	19	15	30	0	0	.275/.335/.388
2018	SYR	AAA	27	95	8	4	0	1	10	10	10	0	0	.250/.337/.333
2018	WAS	MLB	27	143	16	5	0	2	13	16	28	0	0	.232/.322/.320
2019	WAS	MLB	28	31	3	1	0	1	3	3	6	0	0	.250/.323/.393

Breakout: 4% Improve: 38% Collapse: 2% Attrition: 32% MLB: 63%
Comparables: Ryan Hanigan, Dustin Garneau, Bobby Wilson

There are many reasons to despise the present moment in our existence, what with the way our culture has weaponized technology that allows communication to occur instantaneously. Kieboom, though, is a ray of light. In 1976 or some such year, there would be no memorable story to recall of the time everyone thought he had lost a tooth while swinging a bat, and later homered. Without Twitter, the boring but accurate story would have been the first and only story. Furthermore, in 1958 or thereabouts, there would be no combination of two emojis you could send to all fellow Nationals fans to phonetically represent the backup catcher's last name, and signify your excitement about his rare but important contribution to the baseball club — at least not without some artistic skills and serious patience. There would just be a fledgling major leaguer whose highly touted brother is on the way to likely surpass him, and that isn't nearly as fun.

YEAR	TEAM	P. COUNT	FRM RUNS	BLK RUNS	THRW RUNS	TOT RUNS
2017	HAR	2137	0.0	0.4	0.0	0.1
2017	SYR	6418	-4.5	0.5	-0.2	-4.7
2018	SYR	2427	1.3	0.5	0.3	1.8
2018	WAS	5843	-1.4	1.0	0.1	-0.3
2019	WAS	1207	-0.7	0.1	-0.1	-0.7

YEAR	TEAM	LVL	AGE	PA	DRC+	VORP	BABIP	BRR	FRAA	WARP
2016	HAR	AA	25	359	97	6.5	.267	-2.8	C(93): -12.3	-0.6
2016	WAS	MLB	25	1	99	0.5	--	0.2		0.0
2017	HAR	AA	26	70	88	1.0	.200	-0.6	C(19): 1.4	0.2
2017	SYR	AAA	26	176	113	6.5	.320	-0.1	C(45): -3.9	0.4
2018	SYR	AAA	27	95	107	0.2	.274	-1.2	C(21): 2.2, 1B(3): -0.1	0.5
2018	WAS	MLB	27	143	89	2.8	.281	-0.3	C(49): -0.7, 1B(3): 0.0	0.4
2019	WAS	MLB	28	31	96	1.3	.286	-0.1	C -1	0.0

Spencer Kieboom, continued

Batted Ball Distribution

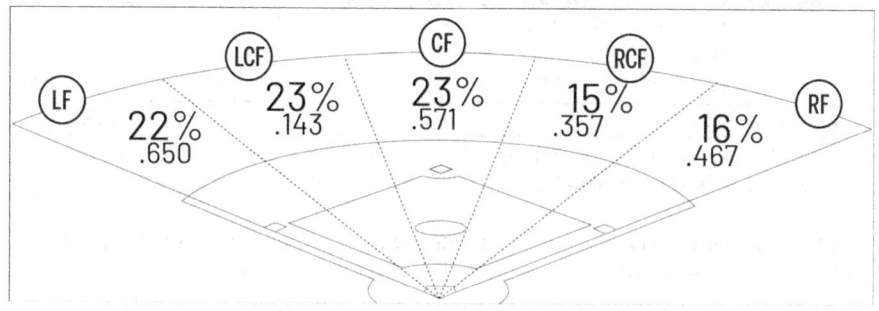

Strike Zone vs LHP

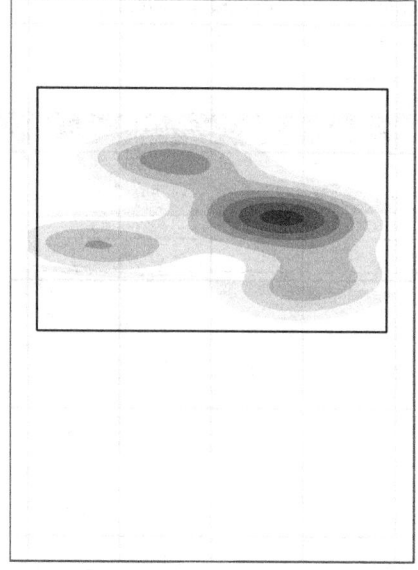

Strike Zone vs RHP

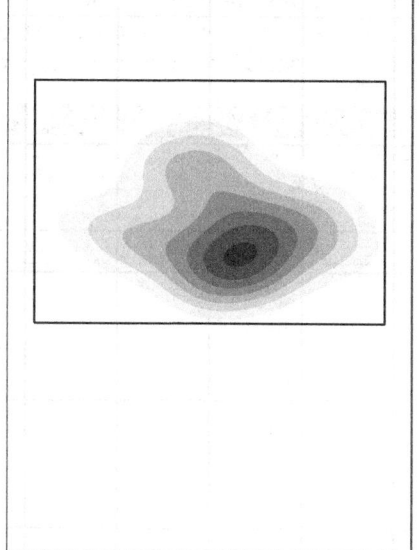

Anthony Rendon 3B
Born: 06/06/90   Age: 29   Bats: R   Throws: R
Height: 6'1"   Weight: 200   Origin: Round 1, 2011 Draft (#6 overall)

YEAR	TEAM	LVL	AGE	PA	R	2B	3B	HR	RBI	BB	K	SB	CS	AVG/OBP/SLG
2016	WAS	MLB	26	647	91	38	2	20	85	65	117	12	6	.270/.348/.450
2017	WAS	MLB	27	605	81	41	1	25	100	84	82	7	2	.301/.403/.533
2018	WAS	MLB	28	597	88	44	2	24	92	55	82	2	1	.308/.374/.535
2019	WAS	MLB	29	607	77	39	2	21	81	66	94	6	2	.287/.371/.487

Breakout: 2%   Improve: 41%   Collapse: 8%   Attrition: 8%   MLB: 99%
Comparables: Kyle Seager, Edgardo Alfonzo, Bill Madlock

Like the cars with TV commercials dedicated to proving they're just as good as name-brand, luxury competitors, Rendon is just as good or better than his name-brand, luxury rivals at third base. Despite your parents' insistence, *Consumer Reports* approvals for reliability and down-ballot MVP votes for steadfast production aren't enough to make an excellent product feel like a lifestyle choice. It's true, all the features you could ever want are there — the extra-base hits, the defense, the fuel mileage. Yet none of those everyday efficiencies instills envy in co-workers on the ride to lunch. Even when they should. Modesty is supposed to be a virtue, right?

YEAR	TEAM	LVL	AGE	PA	DRC+	VORP	BABIP	BRR	FRAA	WARP
2016	WAS	MLB	26	647	115	45.1	.304	0.8	3B(155): -9.0	2.6
2017	WAS	MLB	27	605	139	63.3	.314	2.0	3B(145): -1.6	5.2
2018	WAS	MLB	28	597	134	59.4	.323	2.9	3B(136): -5.7	4.4
2019	WAS	MLB	29	607	129	38.6	.312	-0.8	3B -6	3.0

Anthony Rendon, continued

Batted Ball Distribution

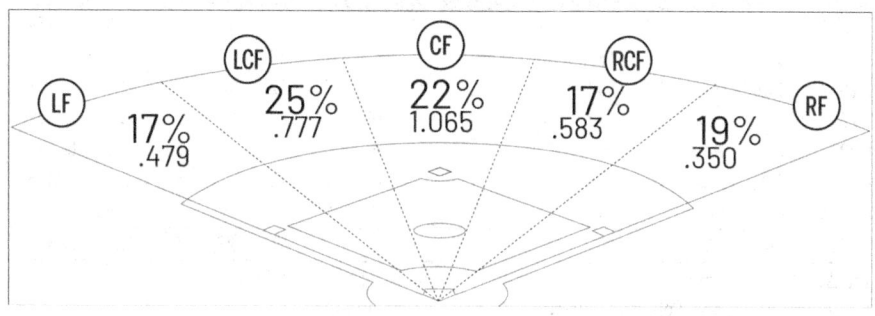

Strike Zone vs LHP   **Strike Zone vs RHP**

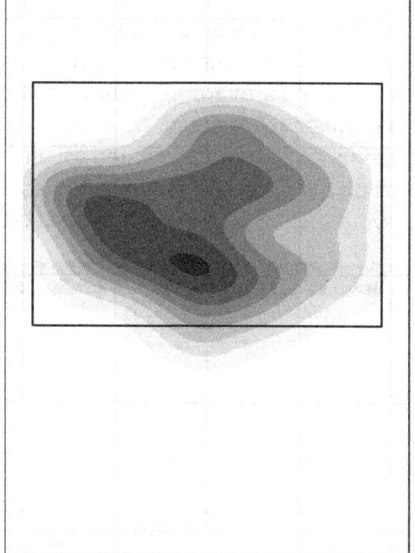

Victor Robles CF

Born: 05/19/97   Age: 22   Bats: R   Throws: R
Height: 6'0"   Weight: 190   Origin: International Free Agent, 2013

YEAR	TEAM	LVL	AGE	PA	R	2B	3B	HR	RBI	BB	K	SB	CS	AVG/OBP/SLG
2016	HAG	A	19	285	48	9	6	5	30	18	38	19	8	.305/.405/.459
2016	POT	A+	19	198	24	8	2	3	11	14	32	18	5	.262/.354/.387
2017	POT	A+	20	338	49	25	7	7	33	25	62	16	7	.289/.377/.495
2017	HAR	AA	20	158	24	12	1	3	14	12	22	11	3	.324/.394/.489
2017	WAS	MLB	20	27	2	1	2	0	4	0	6	0	1	.250/.308/.458
2018	SYR	AAA	21	182	25	9	1	2	10	18	26	14	6	.278/.356/.386
2018	WAS	MLB	21	66	8	3	1	3	10	4	12	3	2	.288/.348/.525
2019	WAS	MLB	22	505	62	23	2	13	52	41	101	22	10	.234/.305/.381

Breakout: 13%   Improve: 52%   Collapse: 0%   Attrition: 21%   MLB: 59%
Comparables: Gregory Polanco, Andrew McCutchen, Dalton Pompey

On September 8, Robles started in center field between Bryce Harper and Juan Soto, and found he was the least accomplished major leaguer in the trio. It was the first time his name had been written on the lineup card in 2018 and, fittingly, the game was delayed. It was supposed to be the year he introduced himself to the wider world, but Robles spent it clawing back from the kind of elbow injury that inspired a "warning: graphic content" on Twitter while everyone gawked at his prodigal teammates. When he re-arrived in Washington, things looked all-systems-go for the anticipated ascension to five-tool, well-rounded star status. A task on the diamond at which Robles does not excel? Still not located, but playing second fiddle could be the first.

YEAR	TEAM	LVL	AGE	PA	DRC+	VORP	BABIP	BRR	FRAA	WARP
2016	HAG	A	19	285	144	31.6	.346	6.2	CF(63): 11.9	3.6
2016	POT	A+	19	198	111	10.3	.304	-1.0	CF(40): 5.9	0.9
2017	POT	A+	20	338	146	30.8	.345	0.7	CF(77): 16.1	3.8
2017	HAR	AA	20	158	136	17.0	.368	2.7	CF(31): 4.1, LF(3): -0.1	1.5
2017	WAS	MLB	20	27	79	-0.6	.333	-0.8	RF(6): 1.2, CF(3): -0.3	0.0
2018	SYR	AAA	21	182	100	9.9	.318	1.2	CF(39): -0.8	0.4
2018	WAS	MLB	21	66	103	5.2	.311	0.7	CF(14): 0.1, RF(2): -0.2	0.3
2019	WAS	MLB	22	505	80	8.6	.266	1.2	CF 9, LF 0	1.7

Victor Robles, continued

Batted Ball Distribution

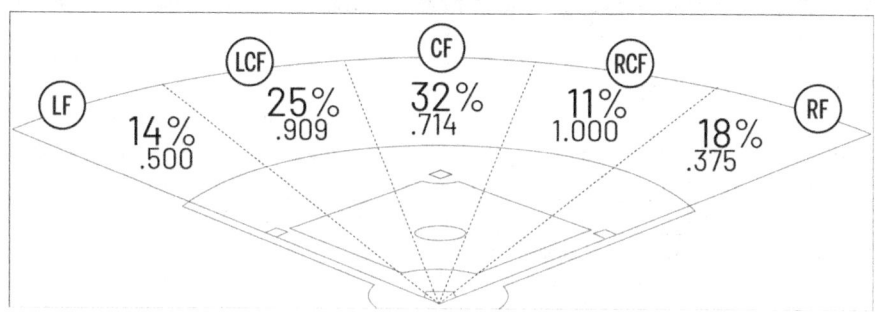

Strike Zone vs LHP   **Strike Zone vs RHP**

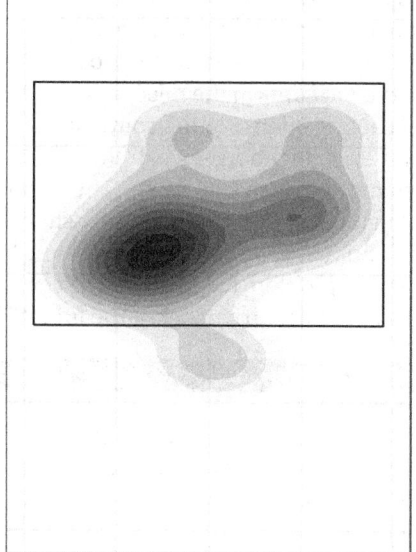

Pedro Severino C

Born: 07/20/93 Age: 25 Bats: R Throws: R
Height: 6'1" Weight: 219 Origin: International Free Agent, 2010

YEAR	TEAM	LVL	AGE	PA	R	2B	3B	HR	RBI	BB	K	SB	CS	AVG/OBP/SLG
2016	SYR	AAA	22	317	25	13	0	2	21	19	45	3	4	.271/.316/.337
2016	WAS	MLB	22	34	6	2	0	2	4	5	3	0	0	.321/.441/.607
2017	SYR	AAA	23	227	17	4	0	5	29	15	43	1	1	.242/.291/.332
2017	WAS	MLB	23	31	0	1	0	0	3	2	10	0	0	.172/.226/.207
2018	SYR	AAA	24	136	14	5	1	6	13	5	23	0	0	.269/.294/.462
2018	WAS	MLB	24	213	14	9	0	2	15	18	47	1	0	.168/.254/.247
2019	WAS	MLB	25	31	3	1	0	1	3	2	6	0	0	.250/.300/.393

Breakout: 16% Improve: 50% Collapse: 5% Attrition: 34% MLB: 78%
Comparables: Curtis Thigpen, Kevin Plawecki, Trevor Brown

Going from "backup catcher of the future" to "backup catcher of the present" is something, one would suppose, and Severino made that small, if short-lived, leap. He logged 213 plate appearances that mostly served to confirm the miserable state of catcher offense in the contemporary game, while producing extremely average defensive numbers. The Nationals' ambitions are too large to actively plan for Severino to get another shot — in fact, they went out and acquired not one but two starting-caliber catchers this offseason — but lack of opportunity is rarely a problem for catchers with even a whiff of big-league ability these days. Back to "backup catcher of the future" it is.

YEAR	TEAM	P. COUNT	FRM RUNS	BLK RUNS	THRW RUNS	TOT RUNS
2016	WAS	1422	-0.4	0.3	0.1	0.0
2017	SYR	8269	8.1	-2.3	0.3	5.2
2017	WAS	939	0.7	-0.4	0.0	0.3
2018	SYR	4103	1.4	0.0	0.0	1.4
2018	WAS	8290	0.3	0.2	0.1	0.5
2019	WAS	1200	0.0	-0.1	0.0	-0.1

YEAR	TEAM	LVL	AGE	PA	DRC+	VORP	BABIP	BRR	FRAA	WARP
2016	SYR	AAA	22	317	96	4.8	.310	-2.0	C(81): -2.0	0.6
2016	WAS	MLB	22	34	110	6.5	.304	0.9	C(15): 0.5	0.3
2017	SYR	AAA	23	227	87	3.3	.280	-0.4	C(58): 5.1	0.9
2017	WAS	MLB	23	31	60	-2.4	.263	-0.5	C(10): 0.3	0.0
2018	SYR	AAA	24	136	94	7.3	.284	-2.1	C(32): 1.1	0.3
2018	WAS	MLB	24	213	61	-7.0	.211	-0.1	C(67): 0.0	0.0
2019	WAS	MLB	25	31	80	0.7	.266	-0.1	C 0	0.0

Pedro Severino, continued

Batted Ball Distribution

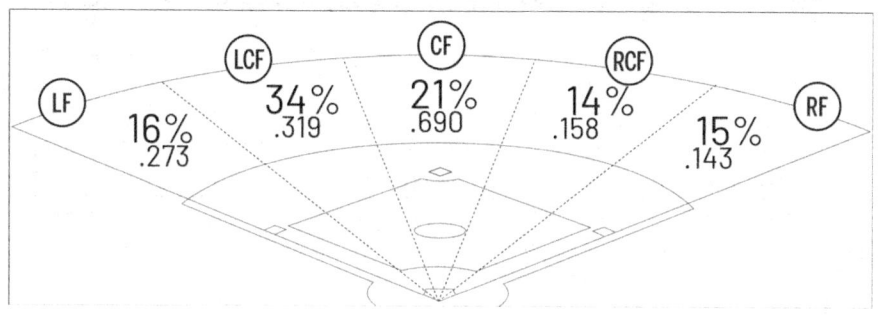

Strike Zone vs LHP

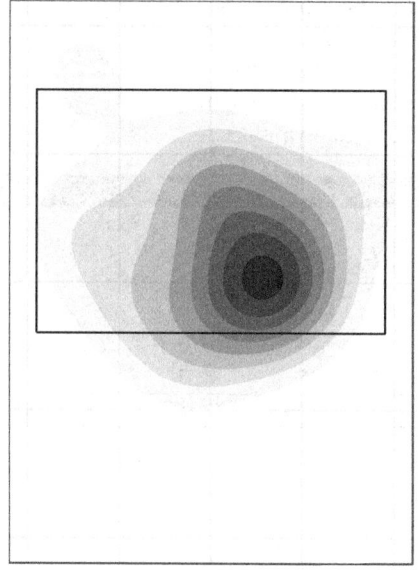

Strike Zone vs RHP

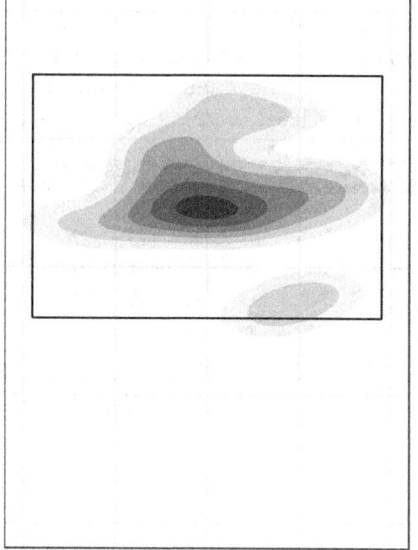

Washington Nationals 2019

Juan Soto LF
Born: 10/25/98 Age: 20 Bats: L Throws: L
Height: 6'1" Weight: 185 Origin: International Free Agent, 2015

YEAR	TEAM	LVL	AGE	PA	R	2B	3B	HR	RBI	BB	K	SB	CS	AVG/OBP/SLG
2016	NAT	RK	17	183	25	11	3	5	31	14	25	5	2	.361/.410/.550
2017	HAG	A	18	96	15	5	0	3	14	10	8	1	2	.360/.427/.523
2018	HAG	A	19	74	12	5	3	5	24	14	13	2	0	.373/.486/.814
2018	POT	A+	19	73	17	3	1	7	18	11	8	0	1	.371/.466/.790
2018	HAR	AA	19	35	4	2	0	2	10	4	7	1	0	.323/.400/.581
2018	WAS	MLB	19	494	77	25	1	22	70	79	99	5	2	.292/.406/.517
2019	WAS	MLB	20	586	78	26	2	23	80	80	125	5	2	.268/.370/.466

Breakout: 22% Improve: 47% Collapse: 1% Attrition: 6% MLB: 53%
Comparables: Bryce Harper, Tony Conigliaro, Mel Ott

Okay, it's Childish Bambino, you know minor leagues are mad whack
Make scouts freak with the sound of my bat crack
Make the nerds think, man, run it, a full season
I crush heaters, I crush sliders, dude, I should be hittin' clean-up
In the majors, with the big boys, O-B-P like Joey V
My age is barely past nineteen, your age is just embarrassing
The chosen one, I rule this world, and now he try to hit like me
My look is like a warning sign, it's all a prelude to my peak

YEAR	TEAM	LVL	AGE	PA	DRC+	VORP	BABIP	BRR	FRAA	WARP
2016	NAT	RK	17	183	198	18.3	.403	1.0	RF(42): 2.9	1.6
2017	HAG	A	18	96	176	8.2	.373	1.0	RF(19): -1.9, LF(2): -0.3	0.7
2018	HAG	A	19	74	214	14.5	.405	0.3	RF(14): 1.1, CF(2): 0.2	1.1
2018	POT	A+	19	73	251	15.4	.340	1.4	RF(14): 1.0, LF(1): 0.0	1.4
2018	HAR	AA	19	35	114	3.6	.364	0.0	RF(4): -0.5, LF(4): 0.6	0.1
2018	WAS	MLB	19	494	125	39.9	.338	-0.5	LF(114): 2.7	3.0
2019	WAS	MLB	20	586	126	36.4	.314	-0.7	LF 1	3.7

Juan Soto, continued

Batted Ball Distribution

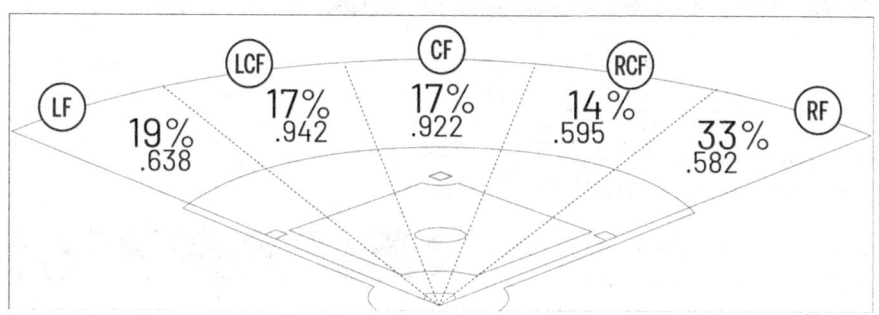

Strike Zone vs LHP

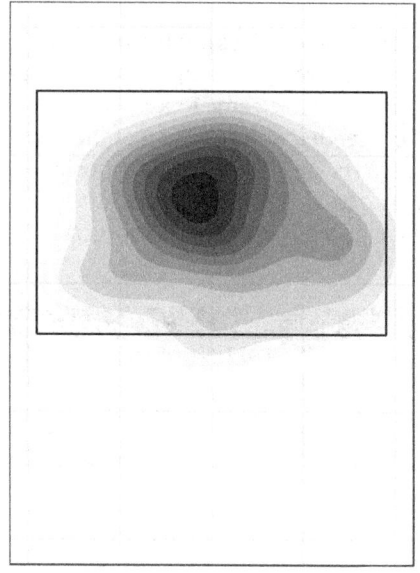

Strike Zone vs RHP

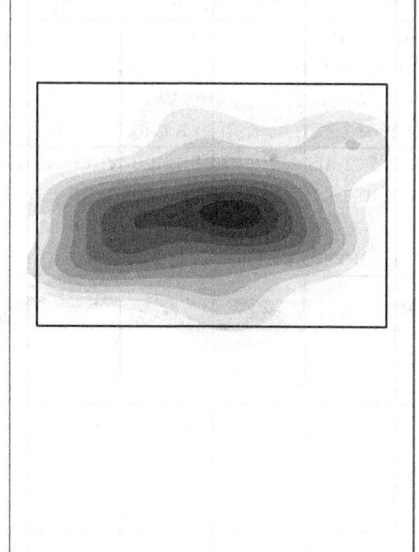

Washington Nationals 2019

Kurt Suzuki C
Born: 10/04/83 Age: 35 Bats: R Throws: R
Height: 5'11" Weight: 210 Origin: Round 2, 2004 Draft (#67 overall)

YEAR	TEAM	LVL	AGE	PA	R	2B	3B	HR	RBI	BB	K	SB	CS	AVG/OBP/SLG
2016	MIN	MLB	32	373	34	24	1	8	49	18	48	0	0	.258/.301/.403
2017	ATL	MLB	33	309	38	13	0	19	50	17	39	0	0	.283/.351/.536
2018	ATL	MLB	34	388	45	24	0	12	50	22	43	0	0	.271/.332/.444
2019	WAS	MLB	35	300	35	16	1	10	39	20	43	0	0	.272/.339/.451

Breakout: 0% Improve: 39% Collapse: 14% Attrition: 20% MLB: 90%
Comparables: Paul Lo Duca, Yadier Molina, Mike Redmond

Suzuki's mid-30s career renaissance kept on trucking with another impressive season, and he was rewarded with more time on the field as he slowly gained more of a lead role over catching mate Tyler Flowers. The poor guy is a magnet for baseballs. He was hit by 13 of them in addition to all the dings he receives behind the plate. He stayed the course and gave the Braves another above-average season at the position. He played his way out of a job with the Twins, came to a rebuilding Braves team as half of a catching duo and proceeded to turn in two of the better years of his career at an age where most catchers are slowing down or losing starting jobs. For his effort, he got a two-year deal to split time behind the plate with Yan Gomes in Washington. Now if we can just get pitchers to appreciate him and stop beaning him in the kidney.

YEAR	TEAM	P. COUNT	FRM RUNS	BLK RUNS	THRW RUNS	TOT RUNS
2016	MIN	13825	-4.7	1.6	-2.5	-6.3
2017	ATL	10594	-0.6	1.4	-0.9	-0.7
2018	ATL	12497	-7.5	1.5	-0.4	-6.6
2019	WAS	9964	-5.2	1.1	-1.0	-5.1

YEAR	TEAM	LVL	AGE	PA	DRC+	VORP	BABIP	BRR	FRAA	WARP
2016	MIN	MLB	32	373	90	6.9	.276	-0.9	C(99): -6.2	0.5
2017	ATL	MLB	33	309	129	27.3	.268	-2.8	C(77): 1.9	2.6
2018	ATL	MLB	34	388	115	25.6	.275	-2.0	C(93): -5.5	1.8
2019	WAS	MLB	35	300	114	17.6	.288	-0.6	C -6	1.2

Kurt Suzuki, continued

Batted Ball Distribution

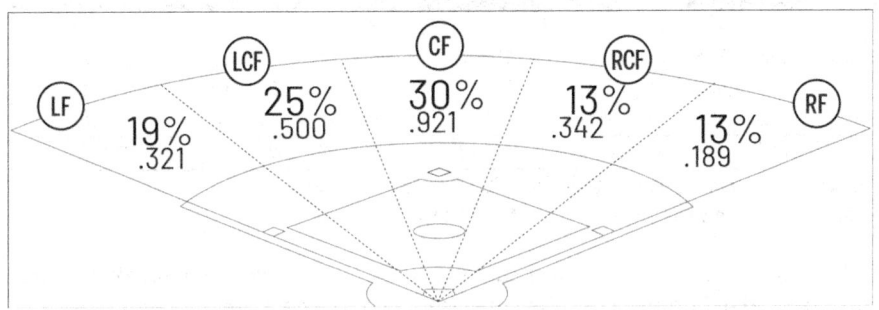

Strike Zone vs LHP

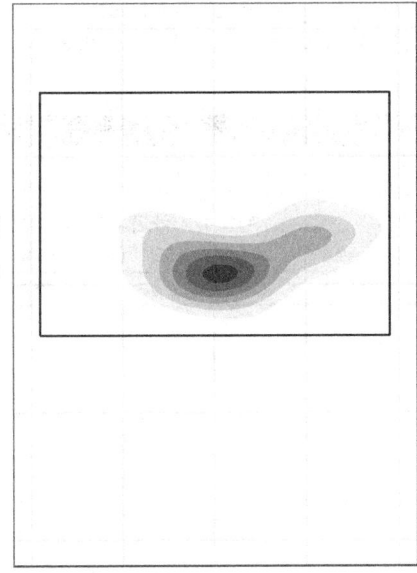

Strike Zone vs RHP

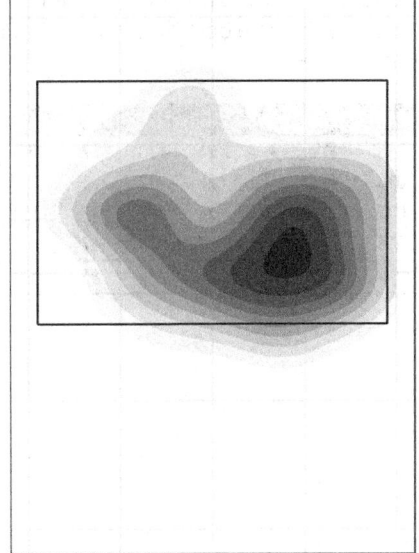

Washington Nationals 2019

Michael Taylor CF
Born: 03/26/91   Age: 28   Bats: R   Throws: R
Height: 6'4"   Weight: 212   Origin: Round 6, 2009 Draft (#172 overall)

YEAR	TEAM	LVL	AGE	PA	R	2B	3B	HR	RBI	BB	K	SB	CS	AVG/OBP/SLG
2016	SYR	AAA	25	130	17	5	1	1	9	12	33	7	1	.205/.285/.291
2016	WAS	MLB	25	237	28	11	0	7	16	14	77	14	3	.231/.278/.376
2017	WAS	MLB	26	432	55	23	3	19	53	29	137	17	7	.271/.320/.486
2018	WAS	MLB	27	385	46	22	3	6	28	29	116	24	6	.227/.287/.357
2019	WAS	MLB	28	259	33	11	1	7	25	21	76	13	4	.226/.293/.370

Breakout: 7%   Improve: 43%   Collapse: 16%   Attrition: 14%   MLB: 95%
Comparables: Drew Stubbs, Peter Bourjos, Mikie Mahtook

Following his second-half power surge in 2017, some expected A. breakout, but 2018 proved A. bummer. Despite supposed gains at the plate, there lingered A. problem. Contact is simply too infrequent when the fleet-footed center fielder swings A. bat, and that's difficult to correct without A. job. Defense remains A. strength, and steals A. certainty. However, the Nationals are not the ideal situation for him as playing time demands are piling up for outfielders A. plenty. It may be that the best thing for Michael A. Taylor's career would be, well, a trade.

YEAR	TEAM	LVL	AGE	PA	DRC+	VORP	BABIP	BRR	FRAA	WARP
2016	SYR	AAA	25	130	72	2.3	.277	2.2	CF(28): 0.5	0.1
2016	WAS	MLB	25	237	71	3.7	.319	0.7	CF(64): 2.9, RF(5): -0.4	0.3
2017	WAS	MLB	26	432	93	26.5	.363	3.1	CF(111): 12.6, RF(2): -0.2	2.7
2018	WAS	MLB	27	385	67	1.2	.320	1.3	CF(113): 8.9, 1B(1): 0.0	0.8
2019	WAS	MLB	28	259	82	4.9	.307	1.6	CF 3, RF 0	0.7

Michael Taylor, continued

Batted Ball Distribution

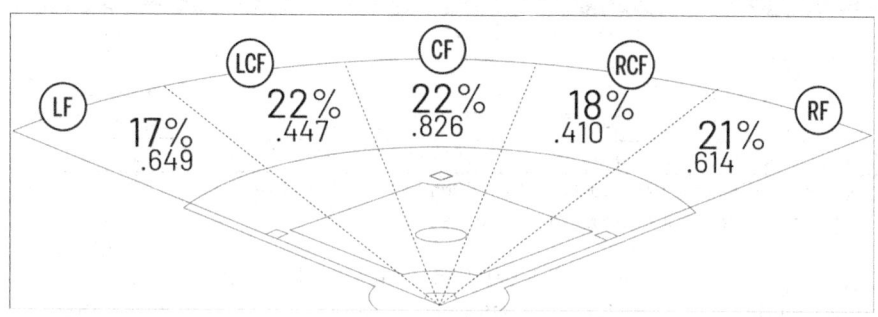

Strike Zone vs LHP   **Strike Zone vs RHP**

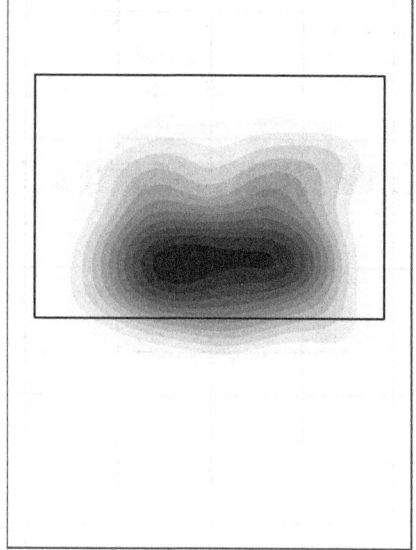

Trea Turner SS

Born: 06/30/93   Age: 26   Bats: R   Throws: R
Height: 6'2"   Weight: 185   Origin: Round 1, 2014 Draft (#13 overall)

YEAR	TEAM	LVL	AGE	PA	R	2B	3B	HR	RBI	BB	K	SB	CS	AVG/OBP/SLG
2016	SYR	AAA	23	371	61	22	8	6	33	37	72	25	2	.302/.370/.471
2016	WAS	MLB	23	324	53	14	8	13	40	14	59	33	6	.342/.370/.567
2017	WAS	MLB	24	447	75	24	6	11	45	30	80	46	8	.284/.338/.451
2018	WAS	MLB	25	740	103	27	6	19	73	69	132	43	9	.271/.344/.416
2019	WAS	MLB	26	625	93	29	5	17	61	51	119	42	8	.270/.335/.429

Breakout: 9%   Improve: 52%   Collapse: 8%   Attrition: 13%   MLB: 98%
Comparables: Bobby Crosby, Josh Rutledge, Aledmys Diaz

It appears Turner has found his level. And what a level it is. Sure, it's not his mind-bending 2016 burst, but he basically repeated his 2017 over 740 (!) plate appearances, with walks becoming a bit more frequent and extra-base hits a bit less frequent. He blazed around the bases in spectacular and efficient fashion. Plus, the defensive metrics say he's grown into a high-caliber asset at shortstop, which means you can expect about 5.0 WARP out of the 25-year-old Turner for the foreseeable future even if he takes no further leap. If you grew up on shortstops who seemed set apart from the rest of the players on the field, a constant threat to alter the game on a dime, Turner just might be your favorite player.

YEAR	TEAM	LVL	AGE	PA	DRC+	VORP	BABIP	BRR	FRAA	WARP
2016	SYR	AAA	23	371	137	40.0	.369	6.1	SS(71): 8.6, CF(6): 0.9	4.2
2016	WAS	MLB	23	324	128	42.1	.388	5.9	CF(45): -2.1, 2B(30): -1.1	2.4
2017	WAS	MLB	24	447	99	36.6	.329	6.8	SS(95): 0.2	2.7
2018	WAS	MLB	25	740	107	45.8	.314	2.7	SS(159): 7.1	5.0
2019	WAS	MLB	26	625	106	34.6	.314	6.1	SS 8	4.4

Trea Turner, continued

Batted Ball Distribution

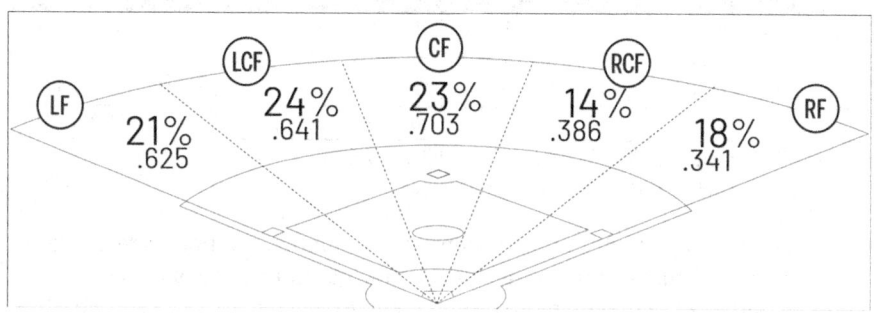

Strike Zone vs LHP

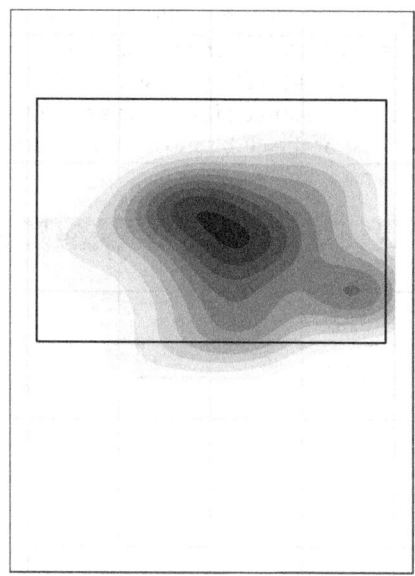

Strike Zone vs RHP

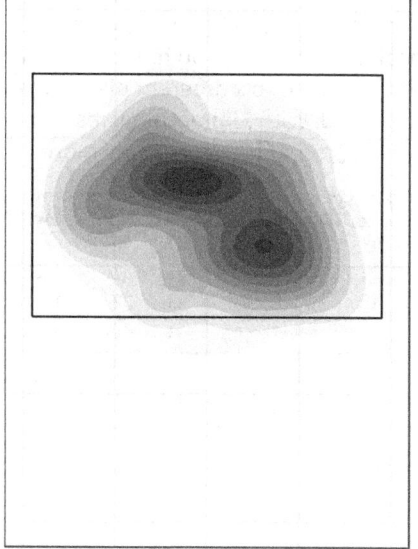

Washington Nationals 2019

Ryan Zimmerman 1B
Born: 09/28/84   Age: 34   Bats: R   Throws: R
Height: 6'3"   Weight: 215   Origin: Round 1, 2005 Draft (#4 overall)

YEAR	TEAM	LVL	AGE	PA	R	2B	3B	HR	RBI	BB	K	SB	CS	AVG/OBP/SLG
2016	WAS	MLB	31	467	60	18	1	15	46	29	104	4	1	.218/.272/.370
2017	WAS	MLB	32	576	90	33	0	36	108	44	126	1	0	.303/.358/.573
2018	WAS	MLB	33	323	33	21	2	13	51	30	55	1	1	.264/.337/.486
2019	WAS	MLB	34	498	59	25	2	20	67	38	106	2	1	.261/.321/.458

Breakout: 1%   Improve: 22%   Collapse: 23%   Attrition: 22%   MLB: 92%
Comparables: Kendrys Morales, Garrett Jones, Hanley Ramirez

The cornerstone upon which the concept of a competitive Nationals team was built years ago, Zimmerman is entering the final guaranteed season of his contract, with an $18 million team option for 2020 unlikely to be picked up. His 2018 started off slow after a bizarre spring training gambit that involved not really training in the spring. He missed all of June but surged in July and August to once again post above-average offensive numbers, continuing a herky-jerky, off-and-on two-year campaign to prove his dreadful 2016 was a fluke. We can accept that premise at this point, and accept Zimmerman for what he is: A declining but still good hitter who plays first base and is likely to miss some time. Applied to a different player, that would be a source of stress or a burden to unload. With Zimmerman, it's an assurance that the club's most familiar face will be around for at least one more year as a new core emerges.

YEAR	TEAM	LVL	AGE	PA	DRC+	VORP	BABIP	BRR	FRAA	WARP
2016	WAS	MLB	31	467	80	-0.5	.248	4.1	1B(114): -2.1	-0.4
2017	WAS	MLB	32	576	130	39.4	.335	-0.3	1B(143): -11.4	1.8
2018	WAS	MLB	33	323	111	14.1	.284	-0.5	1B(73): 1.4	1.0
2019	WAS	MLB	34	498	105	14.5	.293	-0.7	1B -4	0.9

Ryan Zimmerman, continued

Batted Ball Distribution

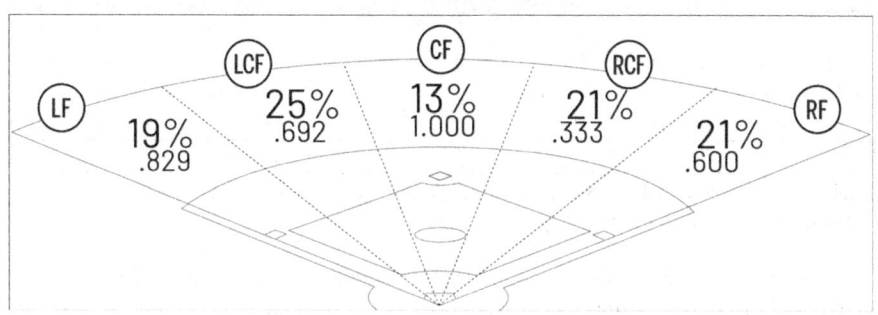

Strike Zone vs LHP   Strike Zone vs RHP

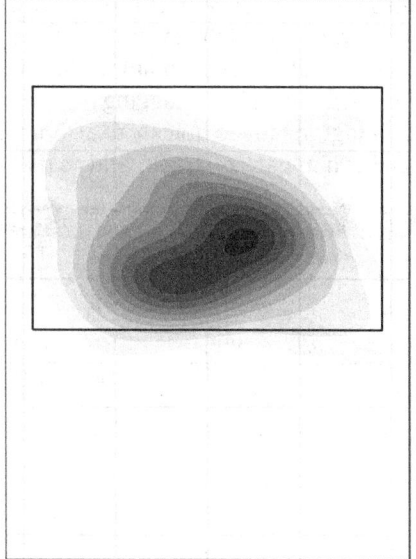

Kyle Barraclough   RHP

Born: 05/23/90   Age: 29   Bats: R   Throws: R
Height: 6'3"   Weight: 225   Origin: Round 7, 2012 Draft (#240 overall)

YEAR	TEAM	LVL	AGE	W	L	SV	G	GS	IP	H	HR	BB/9	K/9	K	GB%	BABIP
2016	NWO	AAA	26	1	0	1	3	0	6	2	0	1.5	13.5	9	46%	.182
2016	MIA	MLB	26	6	3	0	75	0	72^2	45	1	5.4	14.0	113	55%	.301
2017	MIA	MLB	27	6	2	1	66	0	66	53	5	5.2	10.4	76	46%	.291
2018	MIA	MLB	28	1	6	10	61	0	55^2	40	8	5.5	9.7	60	48%	.232
2019	WAS	MLB	29	3	3	2	53	0	56	49	6	5.3	10.1	63	48%	.295

Breakout: 12%   Improve: 43%   Collapse: 31%   Attrition: 18%   MLB: 89%
Comparables: A.J. Ramos, Al Alburquerque, Ryan Cook

In his first couple years with the Marlins, Barraclough thrived with a deadly fastball-slider combo, pitching himself into and out of jams well enough that the team had no choice but to accept his wildness. Last season, however, he backed up. His strikeout rate fell to the lowest mark of his career, his home runs doubled and his walk rate remained the same, which is to say awful. What gives? He introduced a changeup at the expense of his slider. While the changeup played like an average pitch, it was his slider that backed up. As the months progressed, he lowered his release point, which affected the drop of the pitch. Batters recorded the highest slugging percentage against it in Barraclough's career. Washington moved quickly to acquire him this offseason, clearly believing they can get him back on track, wild as that may still be.

YEAR	TEAM	LVL	AGE	WHIP	ERA	DRA	WARP	MPH	FB%	WHF	CSP
2016	NWO	AAA	26	0.50	1.50	1.34	0.2				
2016	MIA	MLB	26	1.22	2.85	2.63	1.9	98.0	54.3	14.3	45
2017	MIA	MLB	27	1.38	3.00	3.55	1.2	96.4	54.2	13	44.7
2018	MIA	MLB	28	1.33	4.20	4.53	0.3	94.8	59.8	12.1	46.8
2019	WAS	MLB	29	1.46	4.05	4.34	0.3	95.6	56.3	13	45.7

Kyle Barraclough, continued

Pitch Shape vs LHH

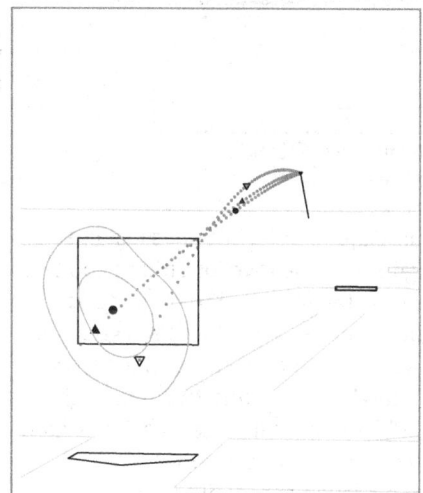

Pitch Shape vs RHH

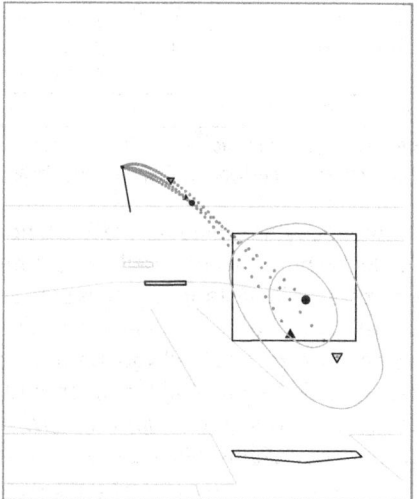

Type		Frequency	Velocity	H Movement	V Movement
●	Fastball	59.8%	94.1 [105]	-3.7 [114]	-13.5 [107]
☐	Sinker				
+	Cutter				
▲	Changeup	11.5%	87.4 [108]	-10.4 [105]	-26.3 [103]
✕	Splitter				
▽	Slider	28.8%	79.4 [77]	11.7 [130]	-44.3 [66]
◇	Curveball				
✥	Slow Curveball				
✱	Knuckleball				
▼	Screwball				

Nationals Player Analysis - 51

Patrick Corbin LHP

Born: 07/19/89 Age: 29 Bats: L Throws: L
Height: 6'3" Weight: 210 Origin: Round 2, 2009 Draft (#80 overall)

YEAR	TEAM	LVL	AGE	W	L	SV	G	GS	IP	H	HR	BB/9	K/9	K	GB%	BABIP
2016	ARI	MLB	26	5	13	1	36	24	155^2	177	24	3.8	7.6	131	55%	.322
2017	ARI	MLB	27	14	13	0	33	32	189^2	208	26	2.9	8.4	178	52%	.326
2018	ARI	MLB	28	11	7	0	33	33	200	162	15	2.2	11.1	246	49%	.302
2019	WAS	MLB	29	12	8	0	29	29	174	153	19	2.9	10.1	195	50%	.298

Breakout: 16%   Improve: 40%   Collapse: 16%   Attrition: 2%   MLB: 94%
Comparables: Anibal Sanchez, Gaylord Perry, Yovani Gallardo

You've seen this movie before. Well, not this *exact* movie, but ones just like it. You know how it'll end: He'll come running for his true love, but it'll be too late. Heartbreak. Devastation. Punch-out. That's Corbin for you. Strikingly good looks aside, Corbin has lived and died by his slider. And the living has been good, as his new contract will tell you. Batters can never seem to decipher the difference between his fastball and his slider until it's too late. That one-two punch got a boost in 2018 as his new-found "slow slider" (you can call it a curve if you want, but he throws it just like his tried-and-true breaker) made a cameo, stole a bunch of strikes and helped tip the odds in his favor, especially early in the count.

YEAR	TEAM	LVL	AGE	WHIP	ERA	DRA	WARP	MPH	FB%	WHF	CSP
2016	ARI	MLB	26	1.56	5.15	5.86	-1.0	94.4	63.8	10.2	44.3
2017	ARI	MLB	27	1.42	4.03	4.92	1.4	94.3	53.3	11.9	43.8
2018	ARI	MLB	28	1.05	3.15	2.74	5.9	93.5	48.6	16.3	41.6
2019	WAS	MLB	29	1.21	3.24	3.51	3.1	93.3	53.4	13.5	43

Patrick Corbin, continued

Pitch Shape vs LHH

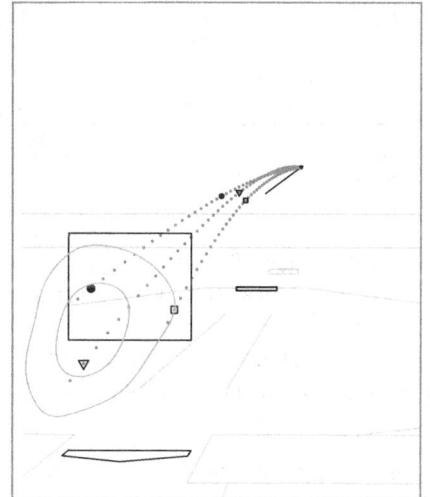

Pitch Shape vs RHH

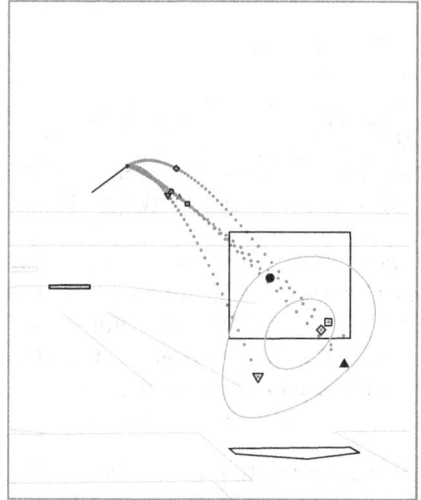

Type	Frequency	Velocity	H Movement	V Movement
● Fastball	19.8%	91.3 [96]	7 [99]	-15.8 [100]
□ Sinker	28.8%	91.3 [94]	13.1 [96]	-19.5 [103]
+ Cutter				
▲ Changeup	1.1%	81.4 [84]	10.3 [105]	-27.1 [101]
× Splitter				
▽ Slider	41.5%	82.1 [89]	-2.6 [90]	-37.3 [87]
◇ Curveball	8.8%	72.8 [79]	-1.4 [73]	-46.5 [103]
✦ Slow Curveball				
✱ Knuckleball				
▼ Screwball				

Washington Nationals 2019

Sean Doolittle LHP
Born: 09/26/86 Age: 32 Bats: L Throws: L
Height: 6'2" Weight: 204 Origin: Round 1, 2007 Draft (#41 overall)

YEAR	TEAM	LVL	AGE	W	L	SV	G	GS	IP	H	HR	BB/9	K/9	K	GB%	BABIP
2016	OAK	MLB	29	2	3	4	44	0	39	33	6	1.8	10.4	45	33%	.281
2017	OAK	MLB	30	1	0	3	23	0	21^1	12	3	0.8	13.1	31	37%	.209
2017	WAS	MLB	30	1	0	21	30	0	30	22	2	2.4	9.3	31	28%	.260
2018	WAS	MLB	31	3	3	25	43	0	45	21	3	1.2	12.0	60	33%	.196
2019	WAS	MLB	32	2	2	29	44	0	46^1	39	7	3.0	11.2	58	36%	.286

Breakout: 21% Improve: 35% Collapse: 34% Attrition: 7% MLB: 95%
Comparables: Jose Valverde, Billy Wagner, Michael Gonzalez

If there were a WARP-like metric for social consciousness, Doolittle might be a Mike Trout-level stalwart atop the leaderboard. An advocate for inclusion and perhaps a more thoughtful ambassador than some of his fellow players deserve, Doolittle has demonstrated that he's well equipped not only to handle the platform he receives as a professional athlete, but also to leverage it to inject some good into the world.

His platform, thankfully, is secure. Though a stress reaction in his foot again ate into his season, Doolittle posted top-level closer numbers. His first full season with the Nationals consisted of 45 innings of sub-2.00 ERA ball, with underlying numbers to support it. Doolittle ran his highest strikeout rate and lowest walk rate since the marvelous 2014 campaign that made his name. To remember that he converted to pitching in pro ball is to remember that, hey, maybe he's still getting better, still honing his craft. Even without huge steps forward, he could soon find himself recognized as one of the game's most renowned closers.

YEAR	TEAM	LVL	AGE	WHIP	ERA	DRA	WARP	MPH	FB%	WHF	CSP
2016	OAK	MLB	29	1.05	3.23	3.75	0.5	97.5	89.3	17	49
2017	OAK	MLB	30	0.66	3.38	2.95	0.5	95.9	87.9	17.5	44.5
2017	WAS	MLB	30	1.00	2.40	3.71	0.5	96.3	87.5	16.8	48.3
2018	WAS	MLB	31	0.60	1.60	2.99	1.0	95.6	88.6	18.9	50.7
2019	WAS	MLB	32	1.15	3.25	3.69	0.6	95.2	87.6	17.6	48.5

Sean Doolittle, continued

Pitch Shape vs LHH

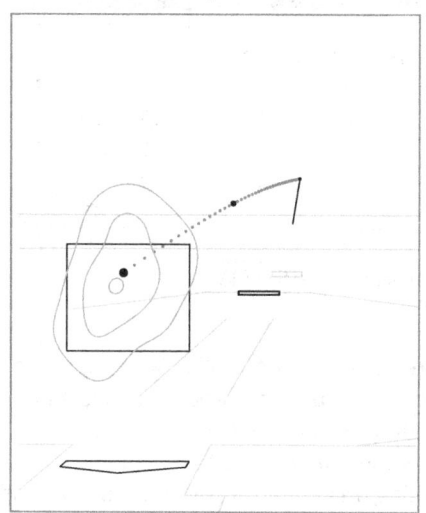

Pitch Shape vs RHH

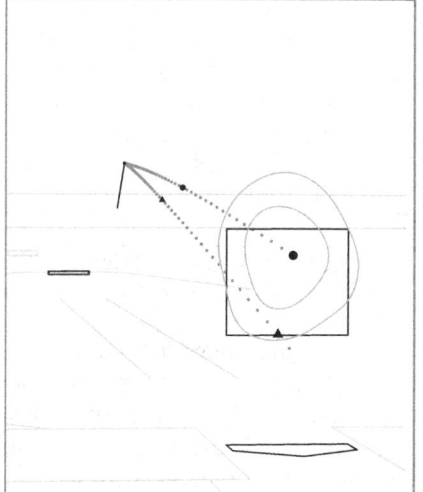

Type	Frequency	Velocity	H Movement	V Movement
● Fastball	88.5%	94.3 [106]	3.1 [116]	-10 [118]
☐ Sinker				
+ Cutter				
▲ Changeup	7.4%	85.6 [101]	12.5 [93]	-19.8 [122]
✕ Splitter				
▽ Slider	4.0%	82.1 [90]	-6.9 [109]	-33.9 [97]
◇ Curveball				
⊕ Slow Curveball				
✳ Knuckleball				
▼ Screwball				

Erick Fedde RHP

Born: 02/25/93 Age: 26 Bats: R Throws: R
Height: 6'4" Weight: 195 Origin: Round 1, 2014 Draft (#18 overall)

YEAR	TEAM	LVL	AGE	W	L	SV	G	GS	IP	H	HR	BB/9	K/9	K	GB%	BABIP
2016	POT	A+	23	6	4	0	18	17	91^2	85	7	1.9	9.3	95	51%	.316
2016	HAR	AA	23	2	1	0	5	5	29^1	33	1	3.1	8.6	28	46%	.360
2017	HAR	AA	24	3	3	0	17	7	56^1	45	4	2.9	8.6	54	52%	.272
2017	SYR	AAA	24	1	2	0	12	6	34	37	3	1.3	6.6	25	62%	.315
2017	WAS	MLB	24	0	1	0	3	3	15^1	25	5	4.7	8.8	15	65%	.426
2018	SYR	AAA	25	3	3	0	13	13	67^1	78	3	2.4	9.4	70	53%	.383
2018	WAS	MLB	25	2	4	0	11	11	50^1	55	8	3.9	8.2	46	54%	.333
2019	WAS	MLB	26	2	2	0	6	6	30	29	4	3.1	8.6	29	49%	.299

Breakout: 16% Improve: 26% Collapse: 24% Attrition: 33% MLB: 61%
Comparables: Chad Green, Shane Greene, Jeff Manship

You would have hoped for Fedde to secure the fifth starter job in Washington in 2018, but that was not meant to be. He got 11 starts in, but about half were after the Nationals had punted on the season. His pitch mix read, uh, like a cry for help — constantly toggling a splitter from show-me offering to real pitch, ditching a cutter, ramping up a slider, leaning on and letting off the sinker that is appears to be his primary weapon on more days than not. Though the league as a whole is moving swiftly away from it, Fedde's best bet at steady innings may be the sinker-slider combo.

YEAR	TEAM	LVL	AGE	WHIP	ERA	DRA	WARP	MPH	FB%	WHF	CSP
2016	POT	A+	23	1.13	2.85	2.45	3.1				
2016	HAR	AA	23	1.47	3.99	3.23	0.7				
2017	HAR	AA	24	1.12	3.04	3.68	0.9				
2017	SYR	AAA	24	1.24	4.76	4.12	0.5				
2017	WAS	MLB	24	2.15	9.39	6.04	-0.1	95.4	61.1	6.7	47.8
2018	SYR	AAA	25	1.43	4.41	3.73	1.4				
2018	WAS	MLB	25	1.53	5.54	4.85	0.3	95.7	54.9	9.5	43.8
2019	WAS	MLB	26	1.35	3.83	4.13	0.3	95.3	57.1	9.1	46.4

Erick Fedde, continued

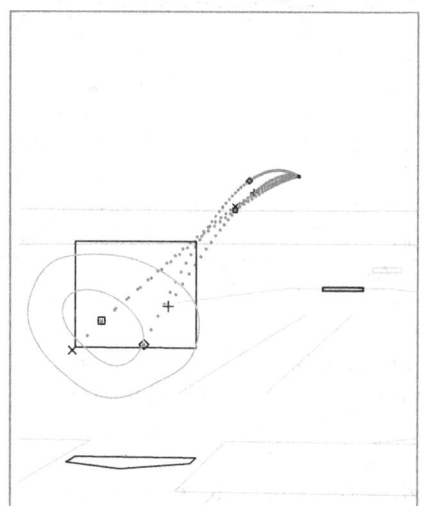
Pitch Shape vs LHH

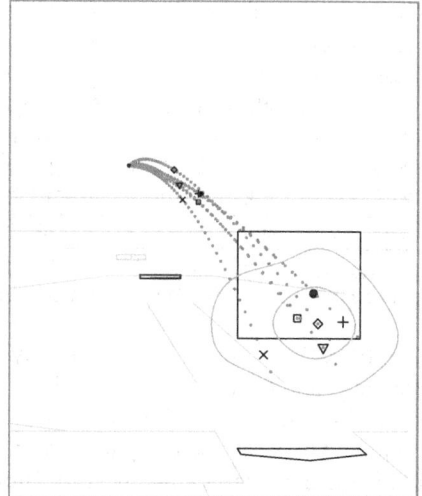
Pitch Shape vs RHH

Type	Frequency	Velocity	H Movement	V Movement
● Fastball	8.1%	93.8 [104]	-5.3 [106]	-19.8 [87]
☐ Sinker	46.8%	94 [107]	-9.6 [125]	-20.8 [99]
+ Cutter	13.5%	88.4 [98]	3.8 [111]	-28.3 [82]
▲ Changeup	1.1%	88.7 [113]	-9.3 [110]	-26.2 [103]
✕ Splitter	10.1%	87.6 [111]	-11.7 [87]	-30.1 [97]
▽ Slider	13.7%	81.7 [88]	8 [114]	-39.6 [80]
◇ Curveball	6.9%	77.6 [97]	9.5 [107]	-47.9 [100]
⊕ Slow Curveball				
✻ Knuckleball				
▼ Screwball				

Koda Glover RHP

Born: 04/13/93   Age: 26   Bats: R   Throws: R
Height: 6'5"   Weight: 215   Origin: Round 8, 2015 Draft (#254 overall)

YEAR	TEAM	LVL	AGE	W	L	SV	G	GS	IP	H	HR	BB/9	K/9	K	GB%	BABIP
2016	POT	A+	23	0	0	2	7	0	9^2	3	0	3.7	14.0	15	59%	.176
2016	HAR	AA	23	2	0	4	17	0	22^1	20	1	2.8	11.7	29	46%	.339
2016	SYR	AAA	23	1	1	2	16	0	24	16	2	1.1	8.2	22	52%	.233
2016	WAS	MLB	23	2	0	0	19	0	19^2	15	3	3.2	7.3	16	42%	.214
2017	WAS	MLB	24	0	1	8	23	0	19^1	20	1	1.9	7.9	17	44%	.328
2018	SYR	AAA	25	1	0	2	8	0	8	7	0	2.2	11.2	10	68%	.368
2018	WAS	MLB	25	1	3	1	21	0	16^1	13	1	5.5	5.0	9	36%	.235
2019	WAS	MLB	26	2	2	1	44	0	46^1	46	6	4.4	8.0	41	43%	.296

Breakout: 20%   Improve: 32%   Collapse: 21%   Attrition: 25%   MLB: 68%
Comparables: Darren O'Day, Daniel Herrera, Jake Barrett

A victim of his own prodigious velocity, a very premature closer label and a shower-related shoulder injury, it feels as though Glover is a disappointment when, in fact, he hasn't had a chance to be ... anything. Yet to eclipse the 20-inning mark in a season, he won't turn 26 until April and is nowhere near being too old for this sh— uh, stuff. Though he struggled in his brief return last season, diminished velocity makes for an easy explanation assuming it gets back to normal over the winter. It seems time is the one thing Glover has never had, and perhaps the only thing he needs to develop into a lethal weapon out of the 'pen.

YEAR	TEAM	LVL	AGE	WHIP	ERA	DRA	WARP	MPH	FB%	WHF	CSP
2016	POT	A+	23	0.72	0.00	2.47	0.3				
2016	HAR	AA	23	1.21	3.22	1.98	0.7				
2016	SYR	AAA	23	0.79	2.25	3.22	0.5				
2016	WAS	MLB	23	1.12	5.03	4.82	0.0	99.0	45.1	12	51.8
2017	WAS	MLB	24	1.24	5.12	2.90	0.5	97.8	37.1	11.3	53.5
2018	SYR	AAA	25	1.12	2.25	2.68	0.2				
2018	WAS	MLB	25	1.41	3.31	6.26	-0.3	97.0	39.2	9.5	47.9
2019	WAS	MLB	26	1.47	4.65	4.81	0.0	97.4	40.7	11	51.6

Koda Glover, continued

Pitch Shape vs LHH

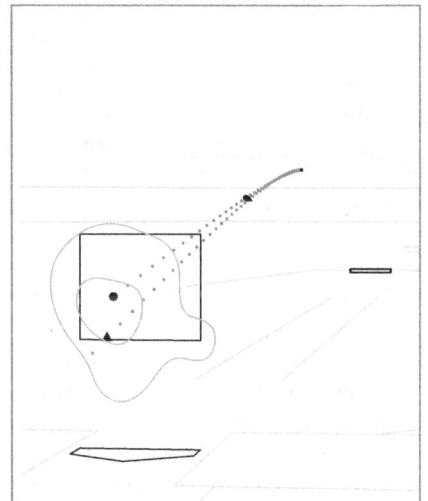

Pitch Shape vs RHH

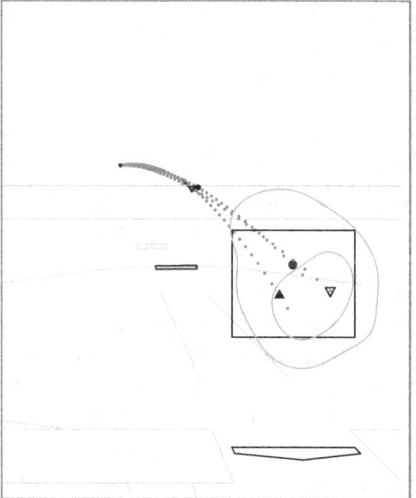

Type	Frequency	Velocity	H Movement	V Movement
● Fastball	39.2%	95.8 [110]	-13.5 [68]	-18 [93]
□ Sinker				
+ Cutter				
▲ Changeup	21.9%	87.2 [107]	-13.8 [87]	-29 [95]
× Splitter				
▽ Slider	29.7%	92 [134]	1.7 [86]	-22.2 [132]
◇ Curveball	9.2%	80.1 [106]	10.2 [110]	-45.7 [105]
⊕ Slow Curveball				
✱ Knuckleball				
▼ Screwball				

Matt Grace LHP

Born: 12/14/88   Age: 30   Bats: L   Throws: L
Height: 6'4"   Weight: 215   Origin: Round 8, 2010 Draft (#236 overall)

YEAR	TEAM	LVL	AGE	W	L	SV	G	GS	IP	H	HR	BB/9	K/9	K	GB%	BABIP
2016	SYR	AAA	27	1	3	1	35	0	47^1	54	1	1.7	6.1	32	66%	.338
2016	WAS	MLB	27	0	0	0	5	0	3	1	0	0.0	12.0	4	67%	.167
2017	SYR	AAA	28	1	3	0	13	1	19^2	21	2	3.7	9.6	21	61%	.345
2017	WAS	MLB	28	1	0	2	40	1	50	50	3	3.2	5.6	31	63%	.294
2018	WAS	MLB	29	1	1	0	56	0	59^2	55	5	2.0	7.2	48	50%	.279
2019	WAS	MLB	30	2	2	0	49	0	51	54	7	3.5	7.4	42	53%	.299

Breakout: 21%   Improve: 44%   Collapse: 22%   Attrition: 12%   MLB: 73%
Comparables: Dan Otero, Brad Ziegler, Kevin Cameron

Only 12 southpaw relievers tossed 50 innings in the majors in each of the past two seasons and, well, you would name at least 10 of them before Grace. But that shortchanges some real work he's done to make himself worthy of those general bullpen innings and not just lefty specialist work. He has long been a worm-killer, but that wasn't enough against righties in 2017, so he boosted his slider usage last year and achieved much more workable ratios (his WHIP against right-handers dropped from 1.41 to 1.11). The lack of strikeouts will always limit his utility in high-leverage spots, but we dare say Grace could remain in that winnowing club of reliable, 50-inning lefty relievers.

YEAR	TEAM	LVL	AGE	WHIP	ERA	DRA	WARP	MPH	FB%	WHF	CSP
2016	SYR	AAA	27	1.33	2.85	3.31	0.9				
2016	WAS	MLB	27	0.33	0.00	2.55	0.1	91.6	76.9	17.9	39.6
2017	SYR	AAA	28	1.47	3.66	3.48	0.4				
2017	WAS	MLB	28	1.36	4.32	6.01	-0.5	92.6	72.2	7.9	50.9
2018	WAS	MLB	29	1.14	2.87	4.45	0.3	92.9	66.9	8.3	54.6
2019	WAS	MLB	30	1.43	4.70	4.84	0.0	92.0	69	8.2	49.5

Matt Grace, continued

Pitch Shape vs LHH

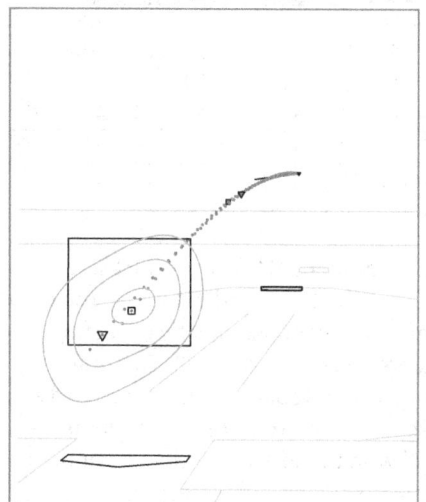

Pitch Shape vs RHH

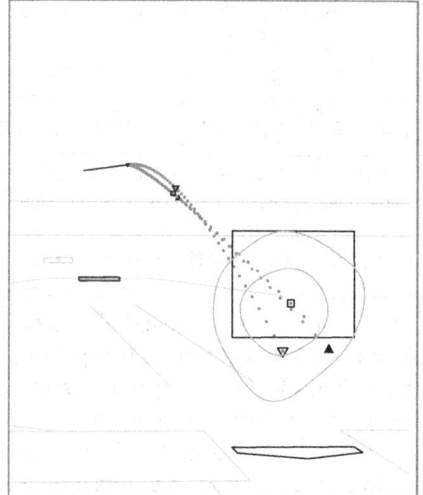

Type	Frequency	Velocity	H Movement	V Movement
● Fastball	0.8%	91.1 [96]	12.7 [72]	-19.7 [88]
□ Sinker	66.1%	91.4 [95]	13.6 [91]	-22.5 [93]
+ Cutter				
▲ Changeup	4.4%	86.1 [103]	13.8 [86]	-27.1 [101]
× Splitter				
▽ Slider	28.7%	82.8 [93]	-3.2 [93]	-34.1 [97]
◇ Curveball				
⊕ Slow Curveball				
✱ Knuckleball				
▼ Screwball				

Jeremy Hellickson RHP

Born: 04/08/87 Age: 32 Bats: R Throws: R
Height: 6'1" Weight: 190 Origin: Round 4, 2005 Draft (#118 overall)

YEAR	TEAM	LVL	AGE	W	L	SV	G	GS	IP	H	HR	BB/9	K/9	K	GB%	BABIP
2016	PHI	MLB	29	12	10	0	32	32	189	173	24	2.1	7.3	154	43%	.274
2017	PHI	MLB	30	6	5	0	20	20	112^1	111	22	2.4	5.2	65	37%	.255
2017	BAL	MLB	30	2	6	0	10	10	51^2	49	13	3.0	5.4	31	36%	.225
2018	WAS	MLB	31	5	3	0	19	19	91^1	78	11	2.0	6.4	65	47%	.252
2019	WAS	MLB	32	5	5	0	16	16	84	85	13	2.6	7.0	66	43%	.288

Breakout: 18% Improve: 43% Collapse: 20% Attrition: 12% MLB: 81%
Comparables: Carlos Silva, Kyle Lohse, Randy Wolf

Rebounding to something resembling his palatable 2016 form, Hellickson provided the Nationals about half a season of much-needed volume in the back of their rotation. He relieved his fastball of some responsibility by collecting strikes on 67 percent of his first pitches, largely via the curveball. Twisting counts in his favor via unpredictability, the former Rookie of the Year closed a one-year deal with a positive WARP, unlike 2012 Rays rotation-mates James Shields, Alex Cobb and Matt Moore. He still won't land any multi-year windfalls like they have at various points, but likely showed enough — despite the foreign-looking 6.41 K/9 — to convince a club with an unsteady rotation to snap him up as a potential flotation device.

YEAR	TEAM	LVL	AGE	WHIP	ERA	DRA	WARP	MPH	FB%	WHF	CSP
2016	PHI	MLB	29	1.15	3.71	3.24	4.6	92.2	58.4	11.6	44.6
2017	PHI	MLB	30	1.26	4.73	5.99	-0.5	91.3	58.4	9.1	45.6
2017	BAL	MLB	30	1.28	6.97	6.97	-0.8	91.6	58.4	8.5	43.9
2018	WAS	MLB	31	1.07	3.45	4.19	1.2	91.5	51.4	9	48.5
2019	WAS	MLB	32	1.27	4.47	4.82	0.2	90.8	56	9.7	46

Jeremy Hellickson, continued

Pitch Shape vs LHH

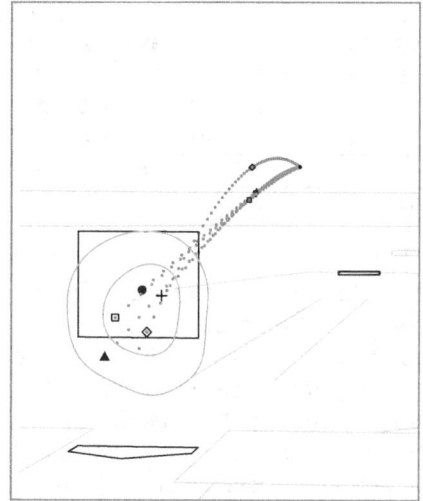

Pitch Shape vs RHH

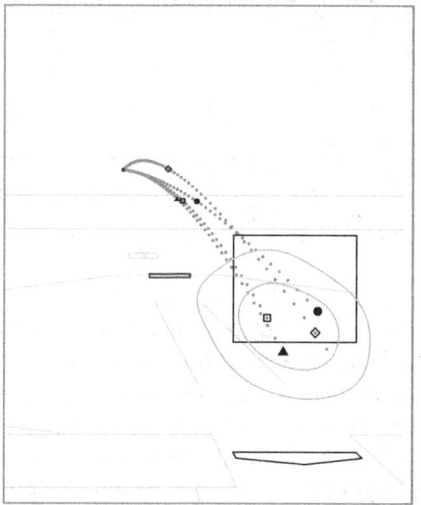

Type	Frequency	Velocity	H Movement	V Movement
● Fastball	16.2%	90.2 [93]	-9.9 [85]	-17.2 [95]
☐ Sinker	24.6%	90.2 [89]	-12.9 [97]	-19.8 [102]
+ Cutter	10.5%	87.5 [93]	-1.6 [80]	-18.9 [119]
▲ Changeup	24.0%	81.7 [85]	-9.3 [111]	-27.8 [99]
× Splitter	1.5%	81.7 [78]	-7.4 [103]	-27.5 [108]
▽ Slider				
◇ Curveball	23.2%	76.9 [94]	7.8 [100]	-53.4 [88]
✥ Slow Curveball				
✳ Knuckleball				
▼ Screwball				

Justin Miller   RHP

Born: 06/13/87   Age: 32   Bats: R   Throws: R
Height: 6'3"   Weight: 215   Origin: Round 16, 2008 Draft (#483 overall)

YEAR	TEAM	LVL	AGE	W	L	SV	G	GS	IP	H	HR	BB/9	K/9	K	GB%	BABIP
2016	ABQ	AAA	29	0	0	0	12	0	12	15	0	3.0	6.0	8	40%	.349
2016	COL	MLB	29	1	1	0	40	0	42^2	50	6	4.2	9.5	45	35%	.367
2017	SLC	AAA	30	5	1	9	38	0	46	50	7	1.6	7.2	37	34%	.307
2018	SYR	AAA	31	2	0	1	9	0	13^2	3	0	2.0	15.1	23	45%	.150
2018	WAS	MLB	31	7	1	2	51	0	52^1	42	10	2.9	10.3	60	35%	.254
2019	WAS	MLB	32	3	2	2	49	0	51	47	8	3.5	9.5	54	37%	.289

Breakout: 15%   Improve: 31%   Collapse: 9%   Attrition: 14%   MLB: 48%
Comparables: Brandon Gomes, Chris Hatcher, Pat Neshek

Uh, I flipped this coin 12 times in a row and gotten tails every time. *Sort of like how journeyman reliever Justin Miller showed up and struck out 31 batters without allowing a run or a walk to start 2018?* No, I totally know what I'm doing. There's a feel to it, the weight turning over on my finger. *See, the trouble with any run of extreme, weird success is —* Tails again! *You start to believe it.* I'm serious, look! I've got this down to a science. *Then reality kicks back in.* Come on, I'm going to a casino! *And for the rest of the season you have, like, a 4.54 ERA.* Damn, it's heads.

YEAR	TEAM	LVL	AGE	WHIP	ERA	DRA	WARP	MPH	FB%	WHF	CSP
2016	ABQ	AAA	29	1.58	6.75	4.08	0.1				
2016	COL	MLB	29	1.64	5.70	6.19	-0.6	95.2	67.1	11.7	50
2017	SLC	AAA	30	1.26	5.48	6.01	-0.4				
2018	SYR	AAA	31	0.44	0.00	3.30	0.3				
2018	WAS	MLB	31	1.13	3.61	4.59	0.2	95.3	70.7	14.1	51.2
2019	WAS	MLB	32	1.30	4.15	4.43	0.2	94.3	68.9	13.2	50.3

Justin Miller, continued

Pitch Shape vs LHH

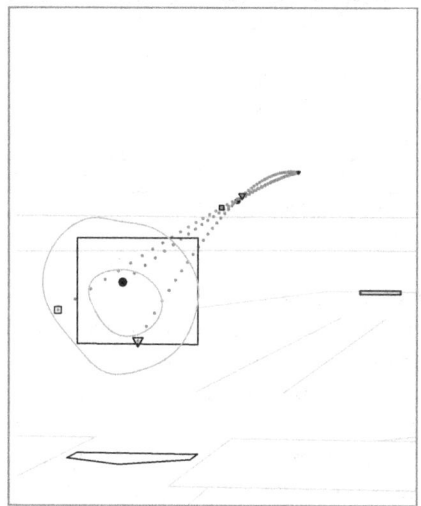

Pitch Shape vs RHH

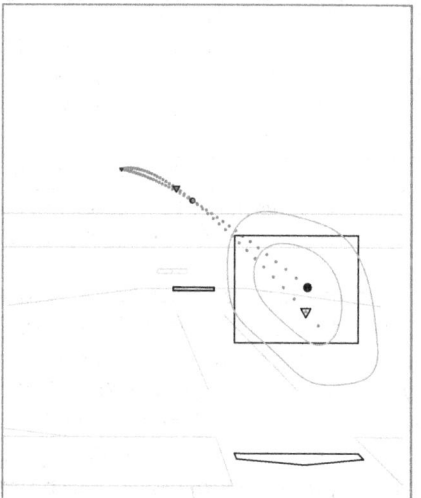

Type	Frequency	Velocity	H Movement	V Movement
● Fastball	65.3%	94.3 [106]	-3.7 [114]	-12.6 [110]
□ Sinker	5.4%	94.7 [111]	-12.2 [104]	-16.3 [113]
+ Cutter				
▲ Changeup	2.0%	90.2 [120]	-11.4 [99]	-19.5 [123]
× Splitter				
▽ Slider	27.2%	86.3 [108]	6.9 [109]	-32.2 [102]
◇ Curveball				
⊕ Slow Curveball				
✶ Knuckleball				
▼ Screwball				

Tanner Rainey   RHP
Born: 12/25/92   Age: 26   Bats: R   Throws: R
Height: 6'2"   Weight: 235   Origin: Round 2, 2015 Draft (#71 overall)

YEAR	TEAM	LVL	AGE	W	L	SV	G	GS	IP	H	HR	BB/9	K/9	K	GB%	BABIP
2016	DYT	A	23	5	10	1	29	20	103[1]	109	9	5.7	9.8	113	39%	.353
2017	DAY	A+	24	2	2	9	39	0	45	21	4	4.4	15.4	77	47%	.230
2017	PEN	AA	24	1	1	4	14	0	17	8	2	5.8	14.3	27	62%	.222
2018	CIN	MLB	25	0	0	0	8	0	7	13	4	15.4	9.0	7	31%	.409
2018	LOU	AAA	25	7	2	3	44	0	51	25	2	6.2	11.5	65	37%	.221
2019	WAS	MLB	26	1	1	0	19	0	20	18	3	7.0	11.2	26	38%	.296

Breakout: 18%   Improve: 31%   Collapse: 7%   Attrition: 20%   MLB: 42%
Comparables: Maikel Cleto, Jose Ramirez, Drew Steckenrider

Minor-league hitters have had absolute fits trying to get hits off Rainey since he transitioned to the bullpen in late 2016, but someone messed with his AI sliders upon getting to Cincinnati, causing batters to destroy his, well, everything. Opposing hitters slugged .880 against his four-seamer and .833 against his slider, which is not ideal when you're basically a two-pitch reliever. Despite the abbreviated recent ugliness, Rainey has the raw stuff to be a high-leverage arm with any notable progress in the command department. Washington believes he can get to that potential, acquiring Rainey in the historic Tanner-for-Tanner swap for Tanner Roark.

YEAR	TEAM	LVL	AGE	WHIP	ERA	DRA	WARP	MPH	FB%	WHF	CSP
2016	DYT	A	23	1.69	5.57	3.93	1.3				
2017	DAY	A+	24	0.96	3.80	1.97	1.5				
2017	PEN	AA	24	1.12	1.59	1.96	0.6				
2018	CIN	MLB	25	3.57	24.43	9.00	-0.3	99.6	71.4	12.2	38.9
2018	LOU	AAA	25	1.18	2.65	3.40	1.0				
2019	WAS	MLB	26	1.64	5.25	5.28	-0.1	99.2	72.7	12.4	39.6

Tanner Rainey, continued

Pitch Shape vs LHH

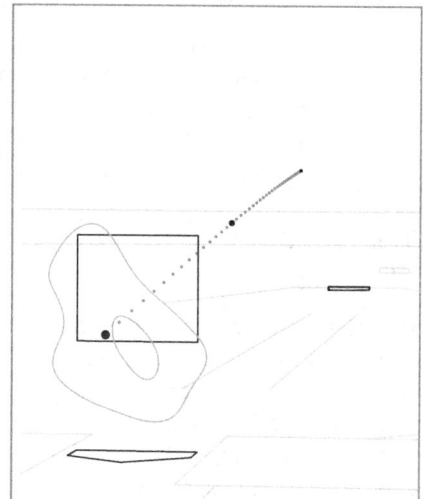

Pitch Shape vs RHH

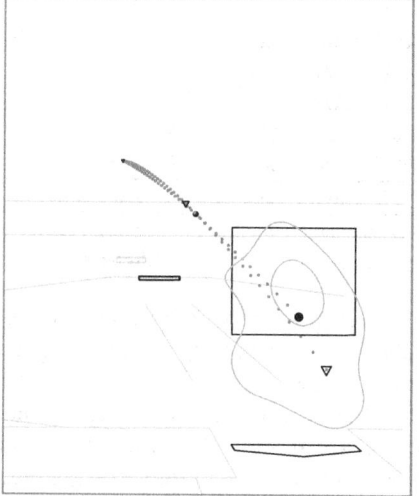

Type	Frequency	Velocity	H Movement	V Movement
● Fastball	71.4%	98.3 [119]	-4.1 [112]	-9.4 [120]
□ Sinker				
+ Cutter				
▲ Changeup	7.9%	90.7 [121]	-7.8 [118]	-17.8 [128]
× Splitter				
▽ Slider	20.6%	89.9 [124]	5.5 [103]	-29.2 [111]
◇ Curveball				
⊕ Slow Curveball				
✳ Knuckleball				
▼ Screwball				

Joe Ross RHP

Born: 05/21/93 Age: 26 Bats: R Throws: R
Height: 6'4" Weight: 220 Origin: Round 1, 2011 Draft (#25 overall)

YEAR	TEAM	LVL	AGE	W	L	SV	G	GS	IP	H	HR	BB/9	K/9	K	GB%	BABIP
2016	SYR	AAA	23	0	2	0	4	4	10^1	14	1	0.9	7.8	9	26%	.382
2016	WAS	MLB	23	7	5	0	19	19	105	108	9	2.5	8.0	93	44%	.319
2017	SYR	AAA	24	2	2	0	5	5	27^2	33	3	2.6	7.2	22	37%	.341
2017	WAS	MLB	24	5	3	0	13	13	73^2	88	16	2.4	8.3	68	41%	.332
2018	SYR	AAA	25	2	0	0	2	2	11^2	12	0	3.1	3.1	4	43%	.273
2018	WAS	MLB	25	0	2	0	3	3	16	17	3	2.2	3.9	7	36%	.269
2019	WAS	MLB	26	4	4	0	13	13	68	71	10	3.3	7.4	57	42%	.296

Breakout: 34%   Improve: 62%   Collapse: 13%   Attrition: 9%   MLB: 90%
Comparables: Erasmo Ramirez, Jeff Francis, Jake Odorizzi

Ross returned from Tommy John surgery to make three starts in September. The takeaways: His fastball velocity was all the way back, sitting in the 93 mph range, and the command that got strong marks in 2017 appeared solid in a small sample as well. What might look different: He used his changeup a *lot* more. Apparently it became a more comfortable pitch during his rehab. The Nationals' rotation options still get bleak after the names in lights, so he'll have an excellent shot at reclaiming a major role if he can shoulder it.

YEAR	TEAM	LVL	AGE	WHIP	ERA	DRA	WARP	MPH	FB%	WHF	CSP
2016	SYR	AAA	23	1.45	4.35	3.88	0.2				
2016	WAS	MLB	23	1.30	3.43	3.99	1.7	95.9	52.5	11.7	47
2017	SYR	AAA	24	1.48	4.88	5.05	0.2				
2017	WAS	MLB	24	1.47	5.01	4.19	1.1	93.8	54.8	11	48.9
2018	SYR	AAA	25	1.37	3.09	6.28	-0.1				
2018	WAS	MLB	25	1.31	5.06	7.08	-0.3	94.6	56	9.2	44.9
2019	WAS	MLB	26	1.41	4.60	4.95	0.1	94.5	54.9	11.3	47.6

Joe Ross, continued

Pitch Shape vs LHH

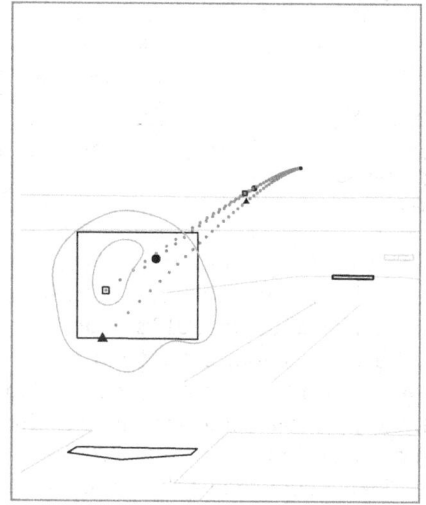

Pitch Shape vs RHH

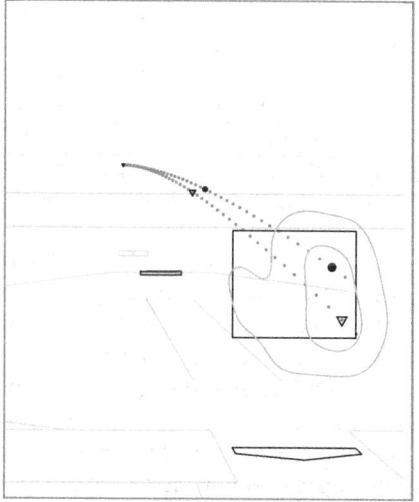

Type	Frequency	Velocity	H Movement	V Movement
● Fastball	31.2%	93.5 [103]	-7.3 [97]	-14.9 [103]
□ Sinker	24.8%	93.4 [105]	-12.6 [100]	-18 [108]
+ Cutter				
▲ Changeup	21.2%	87.8 [110]	-11.5 [99]	-24.5 [108]
× Splitter				
▽ Slider	22.8%	87.1 [112]	2.2 [89]	-26.4 [120]
◇ Curveball				
⊕ Slow Curveball				
✶ Knuckleball				
▼ Screwball				

Anibal Sanchez   RHP
Born: 02/27/84   Age: 35   Bats: R   Throws: R
Height: 6'0"   Weight: 205   Origin: International Free Agent, 2001

YEAR	TEAM	LVL	AGE	W	L	SV	G	GS	IP	H	HR	BB/9	K/9	K	GB%	BABIP
2016	DET	MLB	32	7	13	0	35	26	153[1]	171	30	3.1	7.9	135	41%	.317
2017	TOL	AAA	33	0	2	0	4	4	15[2]	17	3	2.9	11.5	20	46%	.350
2017	DET	MLB	33	3	7	0	28	17	105[1]	139	26	2.5	8.9	104	36%	.354
2018	ATL	MLB	34	7	6	0	25	24	136[2]	106	15	2.8	8.9	135	47%	.255
2019	WAS	MLB	35	9	7	0	23	23	131	127	19	3.0	8.8	128	42%	.295

Breakout: 15%   Improve: 38%   Collapse: 12%   Attrition: 5%   MLB: 80%
Comparables: Josh Beckett, James Shields, Chris Capuano

When life gives you lemons, make lemonade. Or get a playoff start at 34 years old and get knocked around by the Dodgers. Whatever floats your boat. It's not fair to think of Sanchez's NLDS outing when talking about his 2018 season, though. The best years of his successful career seemed long behind him, but he went to Atlanta after being cut by Minnesota in spring training and proceeded to have his best season in at least four years. A key part was simply staying healthy. Another big piece was rearranging his arsenal to become a four-seamer/changeup/cutter guy instead of the typical sinker/slider combo that hitters were keying on the past few years. The cut fastball was the answer to keeping his career alive. That's a plump lemon that he turned into one tasty beverage.

YEAR	TEAM	LVL	AGE	WHIP	ERA	DRA	WARP	MPH	FB%	WHF	CSP
2016	DET	MLB	32	1.46	5.87	5.53	-0.4	93.8	57.4	10.1	47.6
2017	TOL	AAA	33	1.40	4.60	2.71	0.5				
2017	DET	MLB	33	1.59	6.41	6.22	-0.8	92.6	49.6	10.9	49
2018	ATL	MLB	34	1.08	2.83	2.75	4.0	92.4	37.6	11.5	46.2
2019	WAS	MLB	35	1.30	4.03	4.34	1.1	91.7	46.1	10.7	46.7

Anibal Sanchez, continued

Pitch Shape vs LHH

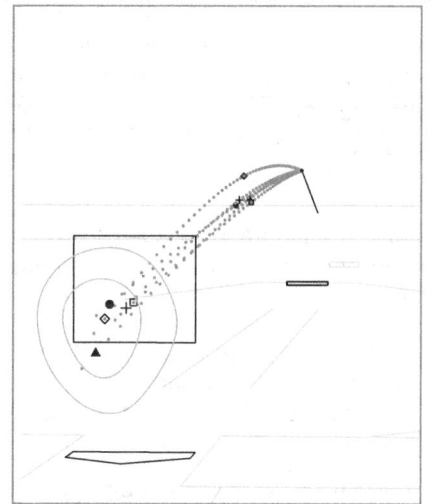

Pitch Shape vs RHH

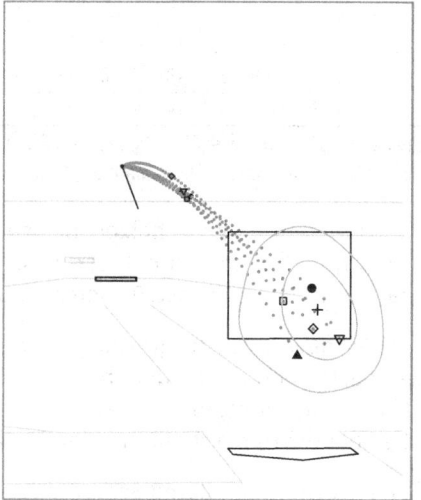

Type	Frequency	Velocity	H Movement	V Movement
● Fastball	29.7%	91 [95]	-2.2 [120]	-14.3 [105]
☐ Sinker	7.9%	91.4 [95]	-9.7 [124]	-16.3 [113]
+ Cutter	23.1%	88.7 [100]	3.9 [112]	-19.6 [117]
▲ Changeup	24.9%	81.3 [84]	-10.3 [105]	-30.9 [89]
✕ Splitter				
▽ Slider	5.5%	83.7 [97]	4.9 [100]	-30.6 [107]
◇ Curveball	8.9%	78.3 [99]	4 [84]	-41.8 [114]
⊕ Slow Curveball				
✳ Knuckleball				
▼ Screwball				

Washington Nationals 2019

Max Scherzer RHP
Born: 07/27/84   Age: 34   Bats: R   Throws: R
Height: 6'3"   Weight: 215   Origin: Round 1, 2006 Draft (#11 overall)

YEAR	TEAM	LVL	AGE	W	L	SV	G	GS	IP	H	HR	BB/9	K/9	K	GB%	BABIP
2016	WAS	MLB	31	20	7	0	34	34	228^1	165	31	2.2	11.2	284	35%	.255
2017	WAS	MLB	32	16	6	0	31	31	200^2	126	22	2.5	12.0	268	38%	.245
2018	WAS	MLB	33	18	7	0	33	33	220^2	150	23	2.1	12.2	300	35%	.265
2019	WAS	MLB	34	14	9	0	31	31	195^1	152	25	2.4	11.3	244	36%	.280

Breakout: 15%   Improve: 43%   Collapse: 25%   Attrition: 3%   MLB: 93%
Comparables: Tom Seaver, Pedro Martinez, Mike Scott

WASHINGTON — Max Scherzer, medical oddity. In a landmark study, researchers report that they have found variants in Nationals pitcher Max Scherzer's genome that confirm he is, in fact, 98 percent husky.

"We knew about the growling," said researcher Cassandra Crisper. "But the pacing, the endurance, and the reluctance to ever surrender a ball are also classic indications." She added, "I don't know how we didn't realize it sooner. The heterochromia should've clued us in years ago."

Researchers compared Scherzer's genome to those of 100 unnamed MLB players, as well as 100 non-athletes, in a genome-wide association study searching for variants associated with competitiveness and muscle endurance. This research, funded by the MLB as well as several anonymous donors, was intended to be the first step toward a comprehensive program of screening all U.S. newborns for these variants, in the hopes of identifying future players as part of an initiative called 'Baby-metrics.' "It's not creepy," said an MLB spokesperson. "I mean, OK, I guess it's creepy. But it was the logical next step now that we're scouting elementary school travel teams."

This research was stymied, however, by the discovery that Scherzer is actually a sled dog in a human suit. "It would explain a lot," said Washington skipper Davey Martinez. "When he talked about the season as the Iditarod, I thought he was being metaphorical. Also, one time, he bit me during the 8th inning when I went to take the ball from him. To be fair, it was a two-hit game—I should have known better."

Dusty Baker, speaking to reporters from his home in San Francisco, said only, "Yes, of course," when asked if he knew about his former ace's unique genetic makeup. A 2017 article from the Washington Post confirms that Baker called Scherzer "a lead dog" for the Nationals, who would go on to win 97 games that season; Scherzer would also win the 2017 Cy Young for his pitching dominance and being 'a very good boy.'

Reporters were also able to reach Matt Williams for comment, who stated that during his tenure as the Nationals' manager, he didn't notice anything different about Scherzer compared to other ace starters he has worked with. Williams was also reportedly unaware of Jonathan Papelbon's 2015 possession by hyena.

YEAR	TEAM	LVL	AGE	WHIP	ERA	DRA	WARP	MPH	FB%	WHF	CSP
2016	WAS	MLB	31	0.97	2.96	2.42	7.7	97.1	55.4	16.7	50
2017	WAS	MLB	32	0.90	2.51	2.32	7.3	95.7	48.7	16.7	48.7
2018	WAS	MLB	33	0.91	2.53	2.29	7.7	96.4	50.1	17.3	50
2019	WAS	MLB	34	1.03	3.09	3.36	3.8	95.2	50.3	16.7	48.8

Washington Nationals 2019

Max Scherzer, continued

Pitch Shape vs LHH

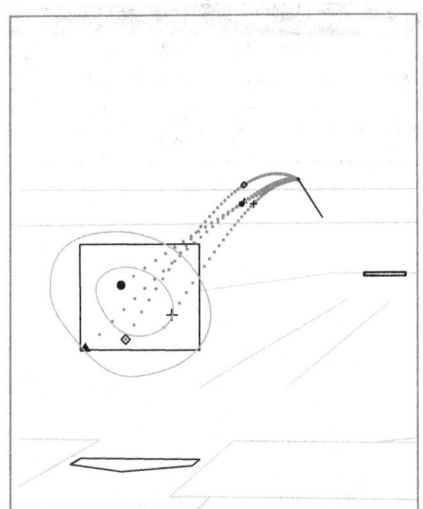

Pitch Shape vs RHH

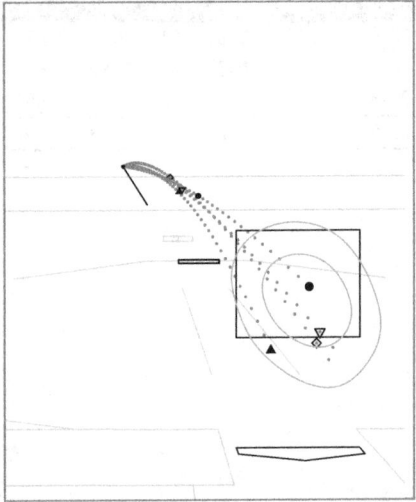

Type	Frequency	Velocity	H Movement	V Movement
● Fastball	50.1%	94.7 [107]	-9 [89]	-15.1 [102]
☐ Sinker				
+ Cutter	10.1%	88.9 [101]	1.8 [100]	-24.4 [97]
▲ Changeup	15.8%	84.3 [96]	-12.8 [92]	-33.1 [83]
✕ Splitter				
▽ Slider	16.0%	85.5 [105]	3.3 [93]	-32.6 [101]
◇ Curveball	8.0%	78.7 [101]	7.5 [99]	-44.9 [107]
⊕ Slow Curveball				
✻ Knuckleball				
▼ Screwball				

Tony Sipp LHP
Born: 07/12/83   Age: 35   Bats: L   Throws: L
Height: 6'0"   Weight: 190   Origin: Round 45, 2004 Draft (#1333 overall)

YEAR	TEAM	LVL	AGE	W	L	SV	G	GS	IP	H	HR	BB/9	K/9	K	GB%	BABIP
2016	HOU	MLB	32	1	2	1	60	0	43^2	52	12	3.7	8.2	40	37%	.323
2017	HOU	MLB	33	0	1	0	46	0	37^1	36	8	3.9	9.4	39	50%	.277
2018	HOU	MLB	34	3	1	0	54	0	38^2	27	1	3.0	9.8	42	42%	.277
2019	*WAS*	*MLB*	*35*	*1*	*1*	*0*	*29*	*0*	*30*	*29*	*5*	*3.9*	*9.3*	*32*	*42%*	*.294*

Breakout: 22%   Improve: 40%   Collapse: 26%   Attrition: 10%   MLB: 88%
Comparables: Kyle Farnsworth, Barney Schultz, Dan Miceli

INTERIOR: *An overlit office at Baseball Gods headquarters.*
"Hey, Valerie. it's Dan down on the 188th floor. Hey...yeah, heck of a game. Anyway, hey, I'm calling about Tony Sipp. Sipp, two P's. Right, middle reliever. Hey, did he… did he make us angry in any way?...Well, it seems that after he signed his big deal with Houston, we made him a REALLY bad pitcher. Like worse than age or general attrition would explain even in the slightest. No…wait. Philip? The data entry guy we fired a while back? No Philip, two P's. Yeah, drunk on the job. No, I know we're always drunk. I mean way too drunk. I thought we caught all his mistakes, but I guess this one slipped through. Yeah. No, I'm just glad we figured it out. Yeah, this is gonna make for a weird stats page for him, but… right. We've done worse. I mean, we all remember Mike Norris. Ugh. OK, great, thanks Valerie. Still on for the Wild Card game tonight at O'Malleys? Great, see you there."

YEAR	TEAM	LVL	AGE	WHIP	ERA	DRA	WARP	MPH	FB%	WHF	CSP
2016	HOU	MLB	32	1.60	4.95	4.12	0.4	93.2	48.2	14	42.9
2017	HOU	MLB	33	1.39	5.79	4.77	0.2	92.2	49.4	13.5	43
2018	HOU	MLB	34	1.03	1.86	2.69	1.0	93.5	52.7	14.7	48
2019	*WAS*	*MLB*	*35*	*1.39*	*4.65*	*4.82*	*0.0*	*91.8*	*49.4*	*13.9*	*44.2*

Tony Sipp, continued

Pitch Shape vs LHH

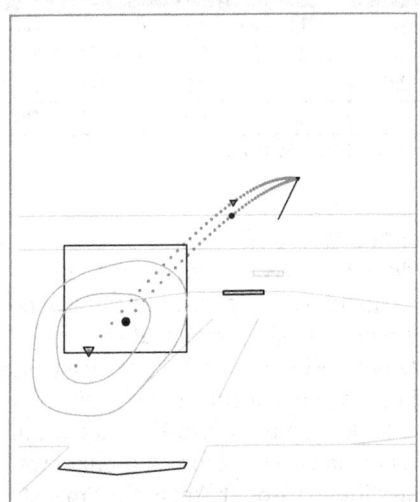

Pitch Shape vs RHH

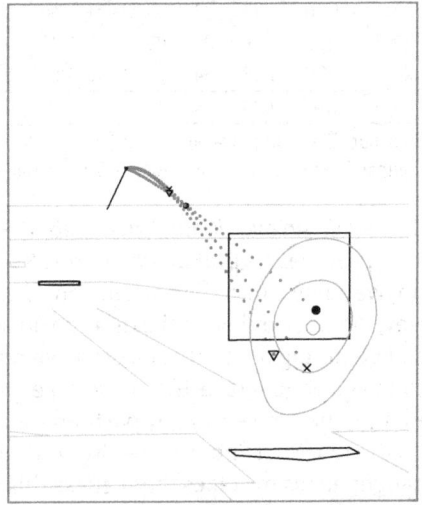

Type	Frequency	Velocity	H Movement	V Movement
● Fastball	52.7%	92.2 [99]	7.3 [97]	-13.7 [107]
☐ Sinker				
+ Cutter				
▲ Changeup				
✕ Splitter	16.6%	79.3 [65]	8.4 [99]	-39.8 [56]
▽ Slider	30.7%	83.2 [94]	0.3 [78]	-34.1 [97]
◇ Curveball				
⊕ Slow Curveball				
✳ Knuckleball				
▼ Screwball				

Stephen Strasburg   RHP
Born: 07/20/88   Age: 30   Bats: R   Throws: R
Height: 6'5"   Weight: 235   Origin: Round 1, 2009 Draft (#1 overall)

YEAR	TEAM	LVL	AGE	W	L	SV	G	GS	IP	H	HR	BB/9	K/9	K	GB%	BABIP
2016	WAS	MLB	27	15	4	0	24	24	147^2	119	15	2.7	11.2	183	42%	.294
2017	WAS	MLB	28	15	4	0	28	28	175^1	131	13	2.4	10.5	204	48%	.274
2018	WAS	MLB	29	10	7	0	22	22	130	118	18	2.6	10.8	156	45%	.309
2019	WAS	MLB	30	11	7	0	26	26	156	131	17	2.8	10.3	179	44%	.293

Breakout: 14%   Improve: 53%   Collapse: 16%   Attrition: 4%   MLB: 97%
Comparables: Ron Guidry, Kenta Maeda, Billy Pierce

A Strasburg word cloud includes many things. Contract, injury, debut, etc. A year after "mold" became an unlikely addition, we can also take note of "cervical nerve impingement" in the orbit. Here's another word that maybe should be more prominently featured: Consistent. Being one of the most electrifying pitching prospects of all time will do this, but every minute detail of Strasburg's career takes on outsized significance. Come to think of it, the same could be said of pitchers who sign giant contract extensions — heaven forbid financial flexibility be at risk. Strasburg, whether he's precisely what you imagined in a 2010 fever dream or not, has put up a DRA- between 51 and 67 in every year of his career. All the way through, since returning in 2012 for his first full campaign, he's started more than 20 games and fired more than 120 innings in each of those seasons. Need a 30-year-old pitcher for the long haul? Strasburg looks like a slam dunk.

YEAR	TEAM	LVL	AGE	WHIP	ERA	DRA	WARP	MPH	FB%	WHF	CSP
2016	WAS	MLB	27	1.10	3.60	2.73	4.5	97.2	57.2	12.3	49.3
2017	WAS	MLB	28	1.02	2.52	2.93	5.2	97.4	51.9	13.8	49.3
2018	WAS	MLB	29	1.20	3.74	2.97	3.5	97.0	52	13	47.2
2019	WAS	MLB	30	1.15	3.16	3.43	2.9	96.4	53.1	13.1	48.3

Stephen Strasburg, continued

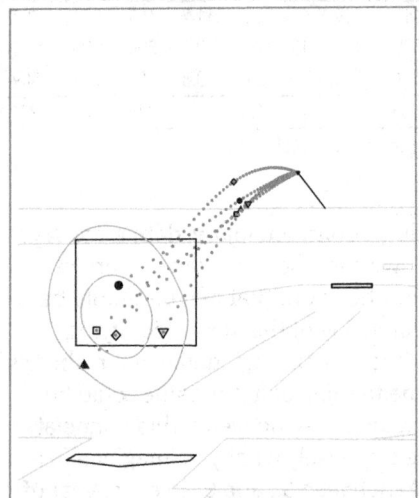
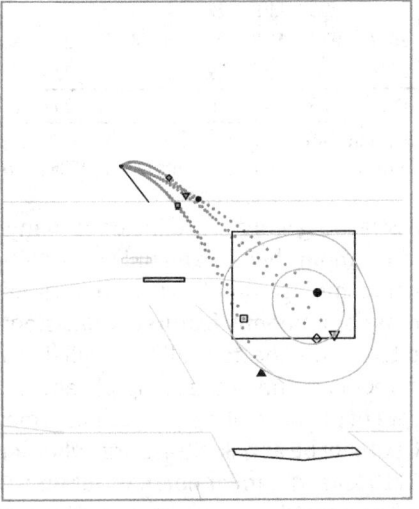

Type	Frequency	Velocity	H Movement	V Movement
● Fastball	44.9%	95.2 [109]	-7.6 [96]	-13.5 [107]
□ Sinker	7.0%	94.4 [110]	-13.7 [91]	-17.8 [108]
+ Cutter				
▲ Changeup	19.9%	88.6 [113]	-13.7 [87]	-27.5 [100]
× Splitter				
▽ Slider	8.6%	88.2 [117]	4.6 [99]	-27 [118]
◇ Curveball	19.5%	82.2 [114]	11.5 [115]	-44.6 [108]
⊕ Slow Curveball				
✱ Knuckleball				
▼ Screwball				

Wander Suero   RHP
Born: 09/15/91   Age: 27   Bats: R   Throws: R
Height: 6'4"   Weight: 211   Origin: International Free Agent, 2010

YEAR	TEAM	LVL	AGE	W	L	SV	G	GS	IP	H	HR	BB/9	K/9	K	GB%	BABIP
2016	HAR	AA	24	3	0	4	39	0	55[1]	53	3	3.4	7.8	48	42%	.316
2017	HAR	AA	25	0	1	10	18	0	23	18	2	2.0	9.0	23	45%	.254
2017	SYR	AAA	25	3	1	10	36	0	42[1]	33	1	3.0	8.9	42	46%	.281
2018	SYR	AAA	26	1	2	1	14	0	17	16	1	2.1	8.5	16	46%	.306
2018	WAS	MLB	26	4	1	0	40	0	47[2]	43	4	2.8	8.9	47	36%	.300
2019	WAS	MLB	27	2	2	0	34	0	36	37	6	4.0	8.7	35	40%	.300

Breakout: 6%   Improve: 14%   Collapse: 20%   Attrition: 23%   MLB: 45%
Comparables: Alan Busenitz, Daniel Stumpf, Jonathan Aro

One Wander Suero, where did he debut? In Washington! It went quite well, really. A sturdy fellow, Suero deployed his cutter about three quarters of the time and came away with almost 50 innings of average-ish relief work. One Wander Suero, where he will find himself in the bullpen pecking order in 2019? The answer might come down to whether he can once again avoid both ground balls and homers at the same time, but his numbers are shockingly consistent by reliever standards.

YEAR	TEAM	LVL	AGE	WHIP	ERA	DRA	WARP	MPH	FB%	WHF	CSP
2016	HAR	AA	24	1.34	2.44	3.02	1.1				
2017	HAR	AA	25	1.00	1.96	3.30	0.4				
2017	SYR	AAA	25	1.11	1.70	3.91	0.6				
2018	SYR	AAA	26	1.18	3.71	3.16	0.4				
2018	WAS	MLB	26	1.22	3.59	4.29	0.3	94.0	79.9	11.9	51.1
2019	WAS	MLB	27	1.46	4.93	5.03	-0.1	93.5	80.8	12.1	51.7

Washington Nationals 2019

Wander Suero, continued

Pitch Shape vs LHH
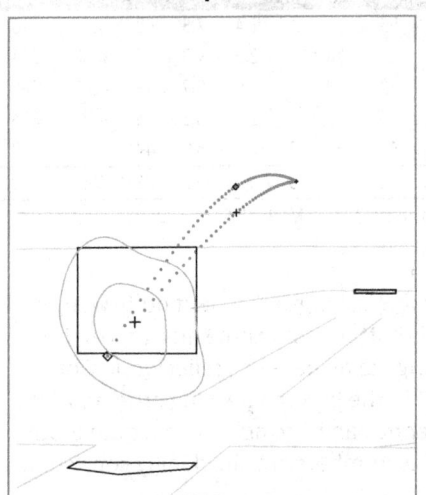

Pitch Shape vs RHH
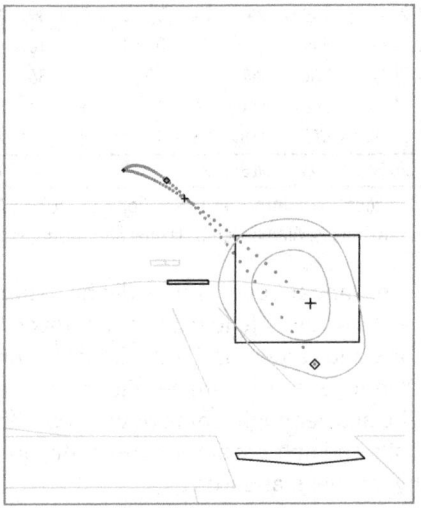

Type	Frequency	Velocity	H Movement	V Movement
● Fastball	4.7%	92.3 [99]	-7.5 [96]	-19.4 [88]
☐ Sinker				
+ Cutter	75.1%	92.1 [120]	3.8 [111]	-19.4 [117]
▲ Changeup	4.5%	88.6 [113]	-7.3 [121]	-25.1 [107]
✕ Splitter				
▽ Slider				
◇ Curveball	15.6%	79.6 [104]	10.3 [111]	-48.8 [98]
⊕ Slow Curveball				
✴ Knuckleball				
▼ Screwball				

Rafael Bautista OF

Born: 03/08/93   Age: 26   Bats: R   Throws: R
Height: 6'2"   Weight: 194   Origin: International Free Agent, 2012

YEAR	TEAM	LVL	AGE	PA	R	2B	3B	HR	RBI	BB	K	SB	CS	AVG/OBP/SLG
2016	HAR	AA	23	607	77	12	4	4	39	45	94	56	10	.282/.344/.341
2017	NAT	RK	24	52	7	2	1	0	3	5	5	2	1	.295/.404/.386
2017	SYR	AAA	24	188	23	9	1	0	11	9	26	7	4	.250/.290/.313
2017	WAS	MLB	24	27	2	0	0	0	0	2	5	0	0	.160/.222/.160
2018	HAR	AA	25	30	0	0	0	0	3	3	5	1	1	.111/.200/.111
2018	WAS	MLB	25	6	1	0	0	0	0	1	0	0	0	.000/.000/.000
2018	SYR	AAA	25	91	11	3	1	1	4	4	23	5	1	.366/.395/.463
2019	WAS	MLB	26	251	30	7	1	5	20	12	52	11	3	.239/.281/.338

Breakout: 7%   Improve: 20%   Collapse: 0%   Attrition: 14%   MLB: 31%
Comparables: Rajai Davis, Jim Adduci, Kyle Hudson

Speed and defense got him two cups of coffee in the majors, but a torn ACL wrecked Bautista's season and modest upward trajectory. He was released to clear a 40-man spot for Adam Eaton's return from injury, but signed back into the system a few days later. He'll need some more realistic on-base skills to stick around—the .500 BABIP from his 2018 Triple-A campaign seems just a wee bit lucky. If he's going to wedge his way into a crowded Nationals outfield situation and build on a brief big-league career, he'll have to revert to the contact-heavy game he showed at lower levels.

YEAR	TEAM	LVL	AGE	PA	DRC+	VORP	BABIP	BRR	FRAA	WARP
2016	HAR	AA	23	607	98	21.9	.333	7.8	CF(102): -3.8, RF(32): 0.2	1.2
2017	NAT	RK	24	52	144	4.0	.333	-0.4	CF(10): -0.8	0.0
2017	SYR	AAA	24	188	76	-0.6	.293	2.7	CF(34): -0.6, LF(7): -0.5	0.1
2017	WAS	MLB	24	27	77	-2.5	.200	0.5	RF(11): -0.4, CF(1): 0.0	0.0
2018	HAR	AA	25	30	59	-3.4	.136	-0.2	CF(6): 0.8	0.0
2018	WAS	MLB	25	6	87	-1.6	.000	0.0	LF(4): -0.1, CF(3): -0.1	0.0
2018	SYR	AAA	25	91	103	7.9	.500	0.0	CF(16): -0.1, LF(2): -0.2	0.1
2019	WAS	MLB	26	251	67	0.0	.282	1.1	CF -1, RF 0	-0.1

Gage Canning OF

Born: 04/23/97 Age: 22 Bats: L Throws: R
Height: 5'10" Weight: 175 Origin: Round 5, 2018 Draft (#161 overall)

YEAR	TEAM	LVL	AGE	PA	R	2B	3B	HR	RBI	BB	K	SB	CS	AVG/OBP/SLG
2018	AUB	A-	21	59	13	3	3	2	7	5	18	0	2	.315/.373/.593
2018	HAG	A	21	128	15	9	0	4	16	11	36	2	0	.223/.294/.411
2019	WAS	MLB	22	251	18	10	0	8	26	9	91	0	0	.147/.177/.289

Breakout: 3% Improve: 6% Collapse: 0% Attrition: 5% MLB: 8%
Comparables: Trayvon Robinson, Daniel Fields, Michael Taylor

The very baseball name Gage Canning might ring a bell for prospect connoisseurs, such as, *hey, he must be the brother of Angels pitching prospect and fellow Pac-12 product Griffin Canning*. Well, prospect connoisseurs, you'd be wrong. Somehow. How?! Anyway, a fifth-rounder in the 2018 draft, Gage blitzed short-season ball despite striking out 30 percent of the time and quickly ascended to Hagerstown. The contact struggles took more of a bite out of his production in a very short sample, but improving in that realm is probably step one in his quest to boost the profile from fourth outfielder to fringe regular.

YEAR	TEAM	LVL	AGE	PA	DRC+	VORP	BABIP	BRR	FRAA	WARP
2018	AUB	A-	21	59	127	7.8	.441	0.0	CF(7): -0.5, LF(5): -0.9	0.1
2018	HAG	A	21	128	94	3.8	.284	-0.2	CF(16): -1.6, RF(14): -1.3	-0.3
2019	WAS	MLB	22	251	17	-17.1	.191	-0.4	CF -1, RF -1	-2.0

Luis Garcia SS

Born: 05/16/00 Age: 19 Bats: L Throws: R
Height: 6'0" Weight: 190 Origin: International Free Agent, 2016

YEAR	TEAM	LVL	AGE	PA	R	2B	3B	HR	RBI	BB	K	SB	CS	AVG/OBP/SLG
2017	NAT	RK	17	211	25	8	3	1	22	9	32	11	2	.302/.330/.387
2018	HAG	A	18	323	48	14	4	3	31	19	49	8	5	.297/.335/.402
2018	POT	A+	18	221	34	7	2	4	23	12	33	4	1	.299/.338/.412
2019	WAS	MLB	19	251	21	4	1	5	20	1	61	1	1	.187/.188/.272

Breakout: 5% Improve: 6% Collapse: 0% Attrition: 3% MLB: 8%
Comparables: Carlos Triunfel, Elvis Andrus, Adalberto Mondesi

Washington's minor-league system is starting to feel a bit like Juilliard and, hello, this could be the next young virtuoso in line behind Juan Soto. Continuing the club's pattern of aggressive placement and promotion, Garcia's precocious talents arrived at High-A shortly after his 18th birthday. He proved himself worthy, harmonizing his contact skills with a bit more pop than he had shown in his pro debut. A shortstop who's already seen some time at second and third base as a result of organizational abundance, this is a triple threat to know early. What with all the other promising talents churning out hits he could one day join a heck of a band.

YEAR	TEAM	LVL	AGE	PA	DRC+	VORP	BABIP	BRR	FRAA	WARP
2017	NAT	RK	17	211	97	7.3	.353	1.7	2B(25): -3.0, SS(17): 0.7	-0.2
2018	HAG	A	18	323	110	16.4	.343	0.7	3B(36): -4.6, SS(27): 0.4	0.4
2018	POT	A+	18	221	116	9.8	.337	-0.3	SS(40): -2.7	0.4
2019	WAS	MLB	19	251	16	-17.4	.221	-0.1	SS -1, 3B 0	-2.0

Carter Kieboom SS

Born: 09/03/97   Age: 21   Bats: R   Throws: R
Height: 6'2"   Weight: 190   Origin: Round 1, 2016 Draft (#28 overall)

YEAR	TEAM	LVL	AGE	PA	R	2B	3B	HR	RBI	BB	K	SB	CS	AVG/OBP/SLG
2016	NAT	RK	18	155	22	8	4	4	25	12	43	1	2	.244/.323/.452
2017	HAG	A	19	210	36	12	0	8	26	28	40	2	2	.296/.400/.497
2018	POT	A+	20	285	48	15	0	11	46	36	50	6	1	.298/.386/.494
2018	HAR	AA	20	273	36	16	1	5	23	22	59	3	1	.262/.326/.395
2019	WAS	MLB	21	251	25	10	0	7	24	14	75	1	0	.178/.226/.318

Breakout: 17%   Improve: 30%   Collapse: 5%   Attrition: 18%   MLB: 38%
Comparables: Franklin Barreto, Willy Adames, Addison Russell

The key boom goes back as far as ancient Rome, and the current run of success dates to the mid-1800s, when Linus Yale Sr. and Jr. invented the flat, metal devices that open your doors, start your cars and jingle in your pockets. Notably, there has yet to be a key bubble or a key bust, and Carter doesn't show many signs of being either. The 2016 first-round pick ascended to Double-A in 2018, strengthened his chances of staying at shortstop and impressed in the Arizona Fall League. A productive big-league career is starting to feel like a lock.

YEAR	TEAM	LVL	AGE	PA	DRC+	VORP	BABIP	BRR	FRAA	WARP
2016	NAT	RK	18	155	84	5.1	.319	-0.3	SS(31): 0.6	-0.1
2017	HAG	A	19	210	159	20.4	.344	-0.7	SS(45): 1.4	2.0
2018	POT	A+	20	285	157	31.4	.332	0.5	SS(56): -0.4	2.3
2018	HAR	AA	20	273	107	13.3	.324	0.5	SS(62): 2.6	1.3
2019	WAS	MLB	21	251	45	-7.4	.222	-0.4	SS 1, 2B 0	-0.7

Raudy Read C

Born: 10/29/93   Age: 25   Bats: R   Throws: R
Height: 6'0"   Weight: 170   Origin: International Free Agent, 2011

YEAR	TEAM	LVL	AGE	PA	R	2B	3B	HR	RBI	BB	K	SB	CS	AVG/OBP/SLG
2016	POT	A+	22	426	54	30	1	9	51	31	53	6	3	.262/.324/.415
2017	HAR	AA	23	442	44	25	1	17	61	27	79	2	0	.265/.312/.455
2017	WAS	MLB	23	11	1	0	0	0	0	0	3	0	0	.273/.273/.273
2018	SYR	AAA	24	52	2	2	0	0	2	1	8	0	0	.260/.269/.300
2018	HAR	AA	24	161	14	9	2	3	24	11	30	0	0	.286/.335/.435
2019	WAS	MLB	25	31	3	1	0	1	3	1	7	0	0	.207/.233/.345

Breakout: 6%   Improve: 23%   Collapse: 0%   Attrition: 16%   MLB: 31%
Comparables: Caleb Joseph, Adam Moore, Luis Exposito

A PED suspension cost Read the first half of 2018, which wound up being a significant missed opportunity. Having made a brief major-league debut in 2017, Raudy and all his friends probably could have come up for a night and gotten a chance at catcher for the Nationals. Read eventually returned with some decent hitting in Double-A, but his first taste of Triple-A was a horror show. It's a toss-up as to whether he remains behind the plate, and perhaps even more of a toss-up as to whether his bat plays well enough to give him a fallback plan.

YEAR	TEAM	P. COUNT	FRM RUNS	BLK RUNS	THRW RUNS	TOT RUNS
2017	HAR	13457	-28.1	1.5	0.4	-27.2
2017	WAS	211	-0.2	-0.1	0.0	-0.4
2018	HAR	4606	-8.1	0.0	-0.2	-8.4
2018	SYR	1432	-2.8	0.0	-0.1	-3.0
2019	WAS	1144	-2.5	0.0	-0.1	-2.6

YEAR	TEAM	LVL	AGE	PA	DRC+	VORP	BABIP	BRR	FRAA	WARP
2016	POT	A+	22	426	120	19.8	.281	-1.9	C(97): 0.7	1.6
2017	HAR	AA	23	442	107	21.8	.290	-3.1	C(104): -24.7	-1.5
2017	WAS	MLB	23	11	72	0.1	.375	-0.1	C(3): -0.4	0.0
2018	SYR	AAA	24	52	80	0.0	.302	-0.1	C(10): -3.1	-0.3
2018	HAR	AA	24	161	115	5.7	.336	-2.5	C(35): -7.8	-0.3
2019	WAS	MLB	25	31	46	-0.6	.278	-0.1	C -3	-0.4

Drew Ward 1B

Born: 11/25/94   Age: 24   Bats: L   Throws: R
Height: 6'3"   Weight: 215   Origin: Round 3, 2013 Draft (#105 overall)

YEAR	TEAM	LVL	AGE	PA	R	2B	3B	HR	RBI	BB	K	SB	CS	AVG/OBP/SLG
2016	POT	A+	21	268	36	16	0	11	32	34	70	0	1	.278/.377/.491
2016	HAR	AA	21	203	19	7	0	3	24	22	51	0	1	.219/.310/.309
2017	HAR	AA	22	480	47	20	0	10	53	55	131	0	0	.235/.325/.356
2018	SYR	AAA	23	61	5	2	0	0	2	7	20	0	1	.185/.279/.222
2018	HAR	AA	23	380	59	16	4	13	56	55	95	1	1	.259/.376/.456
2019	WAS	MLB	24	251	24	9	1	7	28	23	78	0	0	.203/.280/.349

Breakout: 2%   Improve: 11%   Collapse: 0%   Attrition: 10%   MLB: 14%
Comparables: Brock Peterson, Mark Canha, Lucas Duda

The third time was indeed the charm for Ward at Double-A, which he cracked to the tune of 13 homers and a .376 on-base percentage. A former third-round pick whose status as a third-base prospect may soon be a relic, Ward's defensive position is now more often signified with a three in the scorebook. Unfortunately, his numerous connections to that number did him no favors in his first taste of Triple-A. It was only 61 plate appearances, but there was not a three to speak of anywhere in that triple-slash.

YEAR	TEAM	LVL	AGE	PA	DRC+	VORP	BABIP	BRR	FRAA	WARP
2016	POT	A+	21	268	134	19.7	.353	-2.1	3B(49): 2.0	0.9
2016	HAR	AA	21	203	87	1.0	.288	0.9	3B(51): -3.9	-0.3
2017	HAR	AA	22	480	89	10.3	.311	-5.2	3B(114): 3.3, 1B(3): -0.2	-0.2
2018	SYR	AAA	23	61	57	-3.2	.294	-0.2	3B(15): -1.0	-0.3
2018	HAR	AA	23	380	128	21.9	.330	-1.9	1B(82): -0.2, 3B(11): -1.7	0.7
2019	WAS	MLB	24	251	67	-5.4	.273	-0.4	1B -1, 3B 0	-0.7

Austin Adams   RHP

Born: 05/05/91   Age: 28   Bats: R   Throws: R
Height: 6'3"   Weight: 225   Origin: Round 8, 2012 Draft (#267 overall)

YEAR	TEAM	LVL	AGE	W	L	SV	G	GS	IP	H	HR	BB/9	K/9	K	GB%	BABIP
2016	ARK	AA	25	0	1	4	32	0	41¹	29	2	5.2	13.3	61	42%	.321
2017	SYR	AAA	26	6	2	5	44	0	59	44	2	5.6	13.9	91	49%	.321
2017	WAS	MLB	26	0	0	0	6	0	5	4	0	14.4	18.0	10	40%	.400
2018	WAS	MLB	27	0	0	0	2	0	1	1	0	27.0	0.0	0	50%	.250
2018	SYR	AAA	27	1	4	9	41	0	46¹	47	1	3.9	15.2	78	43%	.434
2019	WAS	MLB	28	2	1	0	29	0	30	26	3	5.1	11.5	39	43%	.306

Breakout: 16%   Improve: 18%   Collapse: 21%   Attrition: 26%   MLB: 47%
Comparables: Leonel Campos, Maikel Cleto, John Gaub

Acquired in the Nationals' 2016 shipping out of Danny Espinosa, Adams' first target should be to absorb more innings than the other reliever with his name who tossed 58 innings with the Indians over three seasons. That long may have been the loftiest reasonable goal for the 27-year-old, slider-slinging righty. In 2018, though, he appeared to take a step forward at Triple-A. Adams cut his walk rate from *yikes* to manageable while bumping up an already strong strikeout rate to 37 percent. The result was one of the better reliever profiles in Triple-A. No, not every pitcher with this sort of performance becomes a good major-league reliever, but most of them get some burn. So, maybe Adams can soon improve on his six career innings and move on to a new goal.

YEAR	TEAM	LVL	AGE	WHIP	ERA	DRA	WARP	MPH	FB%	WHF	CSP
2016	ARK	AA	25	1.28	3.05	2.44	1.1				
2017	SYR	AAA	26	1.37	2.14	2.32	1.9				
2017	WAS	MLB	26	2.40	3.60	2.01	0.2	96.2	52.7	14.5	43.7
2018	WAS	MLB	27	4.00	0.00	9.99	-0.1	96.1	58.3	4.2	44
2018	SYR	AAA	27	1.45	3.50	1.24	2.0				
2019	WAS	MLB	28	1.45	3.82	4.16	0.2	95.6	54	12.7	44.1

Washington Nationals 2019

Tim Cate LHP
Born: 09/30/97   Age: 21   Bats: L   Throws: L
Height: 6'0"   Weight: 185   Origin: Round 2, 2018 Draft (#65 overall)

YEAR	TEAM	LVL	AGE	W	L	SV	G	GS	IP	H	HR	BB/9	K/9	K	GB%	BABIP
2018	AUB	A-	20	2	3	0	9	8	31	34	1	2.9	7.5	26	45%	.333
2018	HAG	A	20	0	3	0	4	4	21	23	4	2.6	8.1	19	44%	.306
2019	WAS	MLB	21	2	3	0	8	8	37	42	7	3.9	6.5	27	37%	.311

Comparables: Ranger Suarez, Clay Buchholz, Wilking Rodriguez

The Nationals' second pick in the 2018 draft, Cate is a lefty out of UConn who wields a mean curveball. He likely only fell to the second round because of a forearm injury that cost him time during his final college season, and the team proclaimed itself lucky to snag him. Apparently only impending pro prospects kept the highly competitive and totally ambidextrous Cate from reprising a little trick he pulled in high school — playing the entire season as a right-handed hitter after he had Tommy John surgery on his left elbow.

YEAR	TEAM	LVL	AGE	WHIP	ERA	DRA	WARP	MPH	FB%	WHF	CSP
2018	AUB	A-	20	1.42	4.65	3.82	0.5				
2018	HAG	A	20	1.38	5.57	6.82	-0.4				
2019	WAS	MLB	21	1.56	5.59	6.33	-0.4				

Wil Crowe   RHP

Born: 09/09/94   Age: 24   Bats: R   Throws: R
Height: 6'2"   Weight: 240   Origin: Round 2, 2017 Draft (#65 overall)

YEAR	TEAM	LVL	AGE	W	L	SV	G	GS	IP	H	HR	BB/9	K/9	K	GB%	BABIP
2017	AUB	A-	22	0	0	0	7	7	20^2	18	3	1.3	6.5	15	52%	.250
2018	POT	A+	23	11	0	0	16	15	87	71	6	3.1	8.1	78	47%	.267
2018	HAR	AA	23	0	5	0	5	5	26^1	31	4	5.5	5.1	15	44%	.325
2019	WAS	MLB	24	4	7	0	18	18	83^2	88	16	3.9	7.1	66	43%	.302

Breakout: 4%   Improve: 5%   Collapse: 4%   Attrition: 9%   MLB: 13%
Comparables: Daniel Poncedeleon, James Houser, Scott Barlow

A second-round pick in the 2017 draft coming off Tommy John surgery, Crowe literally moved in next to the Nationals' complex in Florida last winter. Off came the training wheels. Crowe started 2018 at High-A Potomac, tossing 87 exceptional innings and earning a further promotion to Double-A near the end of the year. Those five starts were rockier, but generally confirm the plan: This is a quick-moving starter going into the fine-tuning portion of his development and might land in the back of the Washington rotation by the end of 2020.

YEAR	TEAM	LVL	AGE	WHIP	ERA	DRA	WARP	MPH	FB%	WHF	CSP
2017	AUB	A-	22	1.02	2.61	5.93	-0.2				
2018	POT	A+	23	1.16	2.69	3.35	2.0				
2018	HAR	AA	23	1.78	6.15	4.71	0.2				
2019	WAS	MLB	24	1.48	5.31	6.01	-0.7				

Mason Denaburg   RHP
Born: 08/08/99   Age: 19   Bats: R   Throws: R
Height: 6'4"   Weight: 195   Origin: Round 1, 2018 Draft (#27 overall)

The no. 27 overall pick in the 2018 draft, only a bout of biceps tendinitis kept Denaburg from going even higher. A 6-foot-3 Florida high school righty, Denaburg is straight out of front-line starter central casting. He runs the heater up there at 94, touching 97, with some life. He's got the classic power breaking ball. He apparently even has decent feel for a changeup. He was also born in 1999, so there's a lot of development left to do, but if Denaburg can navigate to his logical endpoint in baseball, his star will surely outshine that of a college football punter, which was apparently also an option for his next athletic venture.

Seth Romero LHP

Born: 04/19/96   Age: 23   Bats: L   Throws: L
Height: 6'3"   Weight: 240   Origin: Round 1, 2017 Draft (#25 overall)

YEAR	TEAM	LVL	AGE	W	L	SV	G	GS	IP	H	HR	BB/9	K/9	K	GB%	BABIP
2017	AUB	A-	21	0	1	0	6	6	20	19	0	2.7	14.4	32	40%	.404
2018	HAG	A	22	0	1	0	7	7	25^1	20	3	2.8	12.1	34	45%	.279
2019	WAS	MLB	23	2	3	0	9	9	35^2	33	5	3.8	9.5	37	38%	.311

Breakout: 3%   Improve: 5%   Collapse: 1%   Attrition: 3%   MLB: 6%
Comparables: Frank Garces, Steven Matz, Christian Friedrich

Sent home from spring training for repeatedly violating rules (curfew, apparently?), Romero is a world-class makeup-problem guy. That exceptional ability to make trouble out of nothing is what got him kicked off the team at the University of Houston, and what allowed the Nationals to draft him several picks after his exceptional pitching abilities might have otherwise warranted. Eventually, he was allowed to report to Hagerstown, but by season's end he had joined a more commonplace club among Nationals draftees: Those who needed Tommy John surgery. If you read the Seth Romero redemption story one day, it will come with a lot of regrettable time and effort burned.

YEAR	TEAM	LVL	AGE	WHIP	ERA	DRA	WARP	MPH	FB%	WHF	CSP
2017	AUB	A-	21	1.25	5.40	1.57	0.9				
2018	HAG	A	22	1.11	3.91	2.52	0.8				
2019	WAS	MLB	23	1.35	4.16	4.72	0.2				

Trevor Rosenthal RHP
Born: 05/29/90 Age: 29 Bats: R Throws: R
Height: 6'2" Weight: 230 Origin: Round 21, 2009 Draft (#639 overall)

YEAR	TEAM	LVL	AGE	W	L	SV	G	GS	IP	H	HR	BB/9	K/9	K	GB%	BABIP
2016	SLN	MLB	26	2	4	14	45	0	40¹	48	3	6.5	12.5	56	53%	.425
2017	SLN	MLB	27	3	4	11	50	0	47²	37	3	3.8	14.3	76	40%	.337
2019	WAS	MLB	29	3	2	5	49	0	51	44	5	4.7	11.7	67	46%	.312

Breakout: 18%   Improve: 42%   Collapse: 42%   Attrition: 12%   MLB: 98%
Comparables: Jonathan Broxton, Francisco Rodriguez, Jake McGee

Washington moved quickly to sign Rosenthal once the offseason began, making a $7 million bet on the former St. Louis closer's return from Tommy John surgery. Prior to going under the knife, Rosenthal was one of the best, hardest-throwing relievers in baseball, frequently lighting up triple digits on radar guns and ranking among the league leaders in strikeout rate. His command and control were weaknesses even before blowing out his elbow, so Rosenthal can't afford to leave much of his overpowering raw stuff on the operating table. If things go well, the Nationals hold a $10 million team option on Rosenthal for 2020.

YEAR	TEAM	LVL	AGE	WHIP	ERA	DRA	WARP	MPH	FB%	WHF	CSP
2016	SLN	MLB	26	1.91	4.46	5.38	-0.2	99.9	77.9	12.8	50.8
2017	SLN	MLB	27	1.20	3.40	2.65	1.3	100.3	74.6	17.1	49
2019	WAS	MLB	29	1.39	3.16	3.61	0.7	99.4	76	15.3	49.8

Austen Williams   RHP

Born: 12/19/92   Age: 26   Bats: R   Throws: R
Height: 6'3"   Weight: 220   Origin: Round 6, 2014 Draft (#184 overall)

YEAR	TEAM	LVL	AGE	W	L	SV	G	GS	IP	H	HR	BB/9	K/9	K	GB%	BABIP
2016	HAR	AA	23	1	7	0	10	10	50^2	66	5	3.9	5.3	30	45%	.339
2016	POT	A+	23	4	6	0	16	16	89^2	113	8	2.6	4.8	48	49%	.337
2017	HAR	AA	24	1	6	0	10	10	46	67	6	2.2	6.7	34	43%	.386
2017	POT	A+	24	2	5	0	9	9	45^1	54	2	2.2	8.3	42	45%	.359
2018	HAR	AA	25	3	3	1	24	2	51^2	34	0	2.3	12.0	69	53%	.281
2018	SYR	AAA	25	0	0	1	8	0	16^1	6	0	2.2	11.0	20	59%	.176
2018	WAS	MLB	25	0	1	0	10	0	9^2	10	5	5.6	7.4	8	23%	.200
2019	WAS	MLB	26	1	1	0	15	0	15	14	2	3.6	9.4	16	44%	.298

Breakout: 6%   Improve: 8%   Collapse: 5%   Attrition: 8%   MLB: 14%
Comparables: Casey Lawrence, Wei-Chung Wang, Artie Lewicki

How many middling Double-A starters see the rope running out and give the bullpen a try? So many! How many double their strikeout rate, power-wash four runs off their ERA and rocket to the majors over the course of a single season? At least one! It remains to be seen if Williams has real staying power as a relief pitcher, but given his status — on the 40-man roster — there's a good chance we'll get to find out. Regardless of the answer, his career got a thousand times more interesting when he stopped starting.

YEAR	TEAM	LVL	AGE	WHIP	ERA	DRA	WARP	MPH	FB%	WHF	CSP
2016	HAR	AA	23	1.74	5.68	4.86	0.1				
2016	POT	A+	23	1.55	5.32	6.18	-0.7				
2017	HAR	AA	24	1.70	6.85	6.10	-0.5				
2017	POT	A+	24	1.43	4.17	4.17	0.6				
2018	HAR	AA	25	0.91	1.39	2.47	1.5				
2018	SYR	AAA	25	0.61	0.55	2.59	0.5				
2018	WAS	MLB	25	1.66	5.59	6.09	-0.1	95.8	53.5	14.4	40.7
2019	WAS	MLB	26	1.31	3.45	3.85	0.2	95.4	54.4	14.6	41.4

Washington Nationals 2019

LINEOUTS

Hitters

HITTER	POS	TEAM	LVL	AGE	PA	R	2B	3B	HR	RBI	BB	K	SB	CS	AVG/OBP/SLG	DRC+	WARP
Telmito Agustin	LF	AUB	A-	21	77	7	2	0	1	5	5	20	1	0	.186/.247/.257	56	-0.7
	LF	POT	A+	21	233	31	10	3	5	30	20	43	7	3	.302/.368/.454	124	1.0
Yasel Antuna	SS	HAG	A	18	362	44	14	2	6	27	32	79	8	7	.220/.293/.331	84	-0.9
Geraldi Diaz	C	DWA	Rk	17	204	20	12	3	1	28	29	31	3	2	.244/.399/.375	135	1.1
Matt Reynolds	SS	WAS	MLB	27	14	1	0	0	0	1	1	4	0	0	.154/.214/.154	67	0.0
	SS	SYR	AAA	27	355	55	31	3	4	29	40	75	2	1	.265/.355/.424	117	1.6
Adrian Sanchez	SS	SYR	AAA	27	295	21	15	2	4	27	16	42	10	6	.234/.281/.349	69	-0.1
	SS	WAS	MLB	27	59	8	2	1	0	3	1	8	0	0	.276/.288/.345	88	0.1
Andrew Stevenson	LF	SYR	AAA	24	331	40	10	1	6	28	31	75	12	6	.235/.318/.338	85	-0.9
	LF	WAS	MLB	24	86	9	2	0	1	13	6	23	1	1	.253/.306/.320	70	-0.2
Chuck Taylor	LF	ARK	AA	24	575	70	25	3	3	60	61	79	2	2	.297/.377/.376	126	0.7
Armond Upshaw	CF	HAG	A	22	419	48	13	1	2	25	42	129	24	9	.234/.317/.292	80	-0.8
Rhett Wiseman	RF	POT	A+	24	478	65	23	4	21	63	63	122	8	2	.253/.361/.484	123	2.6

A 22-year-old from the U.S. Virgin Islands, **Telmito Agustin** was a house on fire for the first five weeks of the season, hitting .386/.411/.659 in High-A before succumbing to yet another injury. It's a hit-tool-led profile, but that will only take him as far as his body and his approach will. ⓣ A shortstop for now, the switch-hitting **Yasel Antuna** took his lumps at Low-A Hagerstown, but maintained a calm, advanced approach at age 18. ⓣ **Geraldi Diaz** will be 18 until July, plays catcher, bats lefty and walked almost as much as he struck out in the Dominican Summer League. ⓣ A power bat taking a part-time stab at returning to catcher, **KJ Harrison** came over from the Brewers in the Gio Gonzalez trade after striking out 147 times in Low-A. ⓣ Brought over from Milwaukee for Gio Gonzalez, **Gilbert Lara** is a 21-year-old infielder and apparent change-of-scenery candidate whose offensive potential has yet to manifest in the low minors. ⓣ **Andruw Monasterio** might have one carrying tool, might have two. But the defensive-minded infielder acquired from the Cubs for Daniel Murphy has a long way to go to make noise in Washington. ⓣ Steve Pearce won World Series MVP. **Ryan Raburn** fell out of baseball, but still sent an unexplained chill down the spine of the left-handed grocery bagger. ⓣ Being purchased by the Nationals freed **Matt Reynolds** from the chronic dysfunction of the Mets, but it also relieved him of nearly all major-league playing time. ⓣ **Adrian Sanchez** won't get demerits for volatility. His Triple-A numbers were nearly identical to 2017, as were his tiny major-league samples. All of them, unfortunately, involved on-base percentages below .300. ⓣ **Moises Sierra** signed a minor-league deal with the seemingly loaded Nationals and then saw his first big-league action since 2014 by the end of April. He was probably as surprised as anyone. ⓥ Entering the season as a 24-year-old, **Andrew Stevenson** needs a serious power surge to keep his prospect light burning. Slugging above .400 in Triple-A would be a start. ⓥ It's not unreasonable to state that **Chuck Taylor** represents the quintessential 2018 Seattle minor leaguer. A speedy, patient outfieder, he'd be considered a viable prospect if he were a few years younger. Or had a little more power, or a little better defense, or, or, or … you get the idea. ⓥ **Armond Upshaw** still struggled with whiffs in his second full pro season, but the Florida junior-college product might be able to outrun any and all concerns you have. ⓥ A return engagement with High-A Potomac, albeit in the summer he turned 24, went swimmingly for **Rhett Wiseman**, as the former third-round pick cranked 21 homers and reached base at a more than acceptable clip.

Pitchers

PITCHER	TEAM	LVL	AGE	W	L	SV	G	GS	IP	H	HR	BB/9	K/9	K	GB%	WHIP	ERA	DRA	WARP
Carlos Acevedo	HAG	A	23	1	4	2	13	3	37[1]	47	7	2.7	8.7	36	43%	1.55	6.51	3.70	0.6
	POT	A+	23	1	3	0	13	1	27[1]	24	2	1.6	6.3	19	40%	1.06	3.62	3.37	0.5
Jacob Condra-Bogan	LEX	A	23	1	1	5	16	0	26	18	2	0.7	13.5	39	42%	0.77	2.08	3.01	0.6
	POT	A+	23	1	2	2	11	0	15	8	0	1.8	7.8	13	53%	0.73	2.40	4.24	0.1
Jimmy Cordero	SYR	AAA	26	4	1	6	41	0	46	43	0	4.3	10.4	53	55%	1.41	1.96	3.10	1.1
	WAS	MLB	26	1	2	0	22	0	19	23	2	5.7	5.7	12	57%	1.84	5.68	6.42	-0.3
Alfonso Hernandez	NAT	Rk	18	2	0	2	13	0	33[2]	29	0	2.1	8.3	31	37%	1.10	2.14	3.42	0.8
	AUB	A-	18	1	0	0	3	0	13	7	0	4.2	6.9	10	33%	1.00	2.77	3.68	0.2
Kyle McGowin	POT	A+	26	1	1	0	2	2	11	8	2	2.5	11.5	14	42%	1.00	4.09	4.47	0.1
	HAR	AA	26	4	3	0	13	13	78	62	7	2.2	10.8	94	50%	1.04	3.69	2.57	2.5
	SYR	AAA	26	3	2	0	8	8	52[2]	26	3	1.5	7.5	44	44%	0.66	1.20	3.15	1.4
	WAS	MLB	26	0	0	0	5	1	7[2]	6	2	5.9	9.4	8	33%	1.43	5.87	4.65	0.0
Vidal Nuno	DUR	AAA	30	3	1	0	8	7	40[1]	38	6	0.7	8.3	37	49%	1.02	3.57	3.63	0.9
	TBA	MLB	30	3	0	0	17	0	33	24	5	2.7	7.9	29	31%	1.03	1.64	4.39	0.2
Jhon Romero	MYR	A+	23	1	2	9	32	0	44	40	1	3.5	11.7	57	36%	1.30	3.27	3.56	0.7
	HAR	AA	23	0	0	0	6	0	7[1]	10	1	3.7	3.7	3	38%	1.77	6.14	5.01	0.0
Sterling Sharp	POT	A+	23	5	3	0	14	14	79[2]	82	4	2.4	6.6	58	62%	1.29	3.16	3.46	1.7
	HAR	AA	23	6	3	0	13	13	68[2]	72	6	3.4	6.2	47	57%	1.43	4.33	4.33	0.8
Jackson Tetreault	HAG	A	22	3	8	0	20	20	110	108	10	2.8	9.7	118	39%	1.29	4.01	4.05	1.5
	POT	A+	22	1	1	0	4	4	22[2]	21	2	2.8	7.9	20	31%	1.24	4.37	3.72	0.4
Austin Voth	SYR	AAA	26	6	8	0	24	24	125[2]	119	13	2.9	8.4	117	42%	1.27	4.37	4.67	1.2
	WAS	MLB	26	1	1	0	4	2	12[1]	12	3	4.4	8.0	11	45%	1.46	6.57	5.14	0.0

Poor looking results—with good peripherals, but a homer issue—at Low-A got 24-year-old righty reliever **Carlos Acevedo** promoted to High-A, where the peripherals ticked down but the results got much better! ⚾ **Jacob Condra-Bogan** has already hit unheralded prospect bingo, having gone unsigned as a late-round pick, discovered an upper-90s heater in indy ball and been dealt for roster filler that everyone will cackle at if he hits it big one day. ⚾ Once traded for Ben Revere, **Jimmy Cordero** ran into every pitching prospect issue around before debuting in 2018 with a Nationals squad that was mainly glad to see he was throwing the ball and not his glove. ⚾ A lefty, **Alfonso Hernandez** pitched most of 2018 as an 18-year-old, making the jump to the U.S. with 31 strikeouts in 33 2/3 innings of Gulf Coast League relief work before a promotion to short-season Auburn. ⚾ If 5-foot-11 reliever and ratio machine **Andrew Istler**, the return from the Dodgers for Ryan Madson, appears in half as many high-leverage situations as Madson did this past October, the Nationals will probably be thrilled. ⚾ A one-time Angels prospect, **Kyle McGowin** blitzed through three levels and reached the majors in 2018, even going four scoreless frames in a spot start before leaving with a blister. ⚾ **Vidal Nuno** still pitches in the major leagues sometimes, but was not even the best Vidal in his own organization last season. ⚾ The son of *the* Mariano Rivera pitched 11 2/3 dreadful innings in the Carolina League before two new lines popped up on his MiLB.com transaction log. *Potomac Nationals placed RHP **Mariano Rivera** on the temporarily inactive list.* And then: *RHP Mariano Rivera retired.* ⚾ A 24-year-old righty reliever acquired from the Cubs for Brandon Kintzler, **Jhon Romero** will now try to take decent strikeout numbers up to the advanced minors. ⚾ Listed four inches taller and 37 pounds lighter than the former NFL receiver, a little more bulk may yet help 22nd-round pick **Sterling Sharp** turn into a major-league starter. ⚾ Big fastball in tow, slender seventh-rounder **Jackson Tetreault** took a crack at his first two levels of full-season ball in 2018 and may have gained a better idea of where his heater is going. ⚾ After a boatload of Triple-A starts and several uneventful call-ups, **Austin Voth** got his first two starts in, both against the Mets, giving up seven runs in one and zero in the other.

Nationals Prospects

The State of the System:
How bad can a system be with two OFP 70s and another likely 101 guy? Let's find out!

The Top Ten:

1 **Victor Robles   OF**   OFP: 70   Likely: 60   ETA: Debuted in 2017
Born: 05/19/97   Age: 22   Bats: R   Throws: R   Height: 6'0"   Weight: 190
Origin: International Free Agent, 2013

The Report: We 8'd him last year, and there's a good argument to do it again. Robles's skills are unchanged, but he keeps getting hurt. Last year, he screwed up his elbow diving for a ball in April and sat out most of the season. In the past, he's also missed time with a hand injury and a few different leg injuries. It's the slightest of knocks, but we hold the role 8 projection in such esteem that we're withholding it this year, even recognizing that we're not going to get another shot to put it out there before he exhausts his eligibility.

Still, Robles is the truest five-tool prospect in baseball, with four tools that could reach 7 or higher, and the power "only" projecting as above-average. He's a natural hitter, combining feel for the barrel with a whip-fast swing. Considering his age-relative-to-league, he's shown excellent discipline and pitch recognition. He's a sure-shot center fielder, with fantastic range, a knack for the big acrobatic play, and a cannon arm. He posts consistent plus-plus times down the line, and will be a major stolen base threat in his twenties; the Nationals carried him more or less as a pinch-running specialist in the 2017 playoffs.

We've been projecting the power to tick up for years now, and it might've finally arrived last September. He should be in Washington's Opening Day lineup and could stay there into the 2030s. Along with division rival Peter Alonso, he's a clear favorite for NL Rookie of the Year.

The Risks: Low, and it would be basically non-existent if not for injuries. He's already had bursts of MLB success, and the profile has an extremely high floor. Unless he's just completely sapped by injuries or something bizarre, he's almost certainly a budding long-term regular. Something to watch for: Although it abated a bit last year, and is a positive skill so far as it affects his OBP, Robles gets plunked really often—he got drilled more times in the minors in 2016 than Brandon Guyer has ever been hit in any MLB season, for example. That increases the injury risk a touch more.

Ben Carsley's Fantasy Take: Don't let prospect fatigue get the best of you; Robles remains a no-doubt top-5 fantasy prospect who could win you leagues as soon as this season thanks to his speed. The injuries are mildly concerning but most are of the freak accident variety, and honestly Robles wouldn't even have to play 162 games every season to have a ton of value. It bears repeating that only 10 players swiped more than 30 bags last season, and only three stole more than 40. Robles can join their ranks, and it wouldn't be too shocking to see him post a line similar to Trea Turner's 2018—.271/.344/.416 with 19 homers and 43 SB—during his peak seasons. Buy, buy, buy.

2. Carter Kieboom   SS   OFP: 70   Likely: 60
ETA: Late-2019 or early-2020
Born: 09/03/97   Age: 21   Bats: R   Throws: R   Height: 6'2"   Weight: 190
Origin: Round 1, 2016 Draft (#28 overall)

The Report: Kieboom goes the prospect dynamite. It was quite a good year for House Kieboom, with Carter's prospect stock soaring in a healthy, fine season and brother Spencer finally joining the international fraternity of backup catchers.

Kieboom's offensive profile is hit-tool oriented, which does bring in some variance. In part, that's because hit tools are inherently variant, but it's also the toughest attribute for scouts to evaluate. He does have plus raw power, which started showing up in games, and he has the sort of bat speed you associate with good averages and plenty of doubles. His performance in Double-A looks sort of ugly on the triple-slash, and he does need to improve his pitch recognition to succeed in the upper minors and majors. Yet by DRC+ he was still close to a league-average bat as a 20-year-old in his first taste of Double-A. That's not a negative, especially if he improves during his second spin through the Eastern League.

Out in the field, we have greater hope that he might stick at shortstop than we used to. He's retained more athleticism and nimbleness than we thought, and migrated from the "probably not" bucket to the "maybe" bucket at shortstop. We also now suspect that he might end up moving to second instead of third if he slides down the spectrum, which would be slight added value in a vacuum and might matter a ton if the Nats re-sign Anthony Rendon.

The Risks: Medium. We'd like to see him hit for average at higher levels. Health has been an issue. He could still slide down the defensive spectrum.

Ben Carsley's Fantasy Take: Kieboom has a bit of an odd profile as a guy who's perhaps a safer bet to hit .280-plus than he is to hit 20-plus bombs yearly, but that's not necessarily a bad thing as long as he remains shortstop-eligible.

There's no true fantasy star upside here, but Kieboom could be a top-10 producer at the position through much of his 20s before perhaps settling in as a top-15 third baseman (and hopefully growing into a bit more pop) later in his career. He's hardly an unknown at this point, but I still think he's a bit undervalued in dynasty circles.

3. Luis Garcia   SS
OFP: 60   **Likely:** 50   **ETA:** 2020
Born: 05/16/00   Age: 19   Bats: L   Throws: R   Height: 6'0"   Weight: 190
Origin: International Free Agent, 2016

The Report: I've sat on Garcia often enough that I should have a good handle on him, as he rolled through Lakewood twice while with Hagerstown. But if I'm being entirely honest, I didn't "see" it. He only played shortstop once between the two series, and while he was fine everywhere and even flashy sometimes, you usually don't project guys as MLB shortstops if they're playing more third than short in the Sally. His swing looked a bit stiff and I just didn't see him as more than a garden variety good prospect.

What could I have missed? Garcia was often playing out of position to increase his versatility and to let Yasel Antuna take shortstop reps. Maybe he didn't show great for me because of minor injuries. Maybe he was working on something specific, trying out a swing adjustment for a few weeks. Maybe he just had a bad group of games—it happens, and sometimes we don't think about that enough when filing.

The rest of the story should color this too: Everyone else I have talked to about Luis Garcia likes his offensive potential. You know the terms: a quick bat, a smooth stroke, some power projection, advanced ability for his age, that sort of stuff. He turned 18 a month into a season in which he played well at both full-season A-ball levels. The defensive consensus is still that he sticks at shortstop, but even if he lands elsewhere he still projects to add real defensive value. He's quite athletic and the body has good projectability. He's a seven-figure former IFA, and while bonus numbers aren't necessarily important, they are a good indicator that he was a well-regarded 14-year-old. This isn't a pref list based on my live looks and little else, and the preponderance of the evidence points to Garcia as a 101 candidate and the clear third-best guy in this system.

The Risks: Low, considering his age. The Nationals have been well-served by moving prospects extremely aggressively, and Garcia has responded to it well already. He has a real shot to be in the majors as a teenager.

Ben Carsley's Fantasy Take: Hey Jarrett, how about you fight me? Garcia is one of my absolute favorite dynasty prospects: I was so unreasonably high on him in the first draft of last off-season's top-101 that BP podcast personality Craig Goldstein genuinely questioned my sanity (for not the first or last time). But if you listened and went all-in on him a year ago, you're pretty happy right now. Garcia's MLB ETA may be a bit more generous than his fantasy impact ETA, but in his prime we're talking about a well-rounded top-10 shortstop who could challenge for 20/20 status. I am Brick in the "do you really love lamp" scene, and Garcia is lamp.

4. Mason Denaburg   RHP   OFP: 55   Likely: 45   ETA: 2023
Born: 08/08/99   Age: 19   Bats: R   Throws: R   Height: 6'4"   Weight: 195
Origin: Round 1, 2018 Draft (#27 overall)

The Report: We normally try to avoid ranking prep arms who don't pitch much before or after the draft because of bicep problems, but this isn't a very good system and Denaburg's arm is more interesting than most. Once a candidate to be the first prep hurler selected, the righty never pitched after signing, although he did throw in instructs. (You'll be shocked to hear that the Nationals drafted a Boras client who fell due to injuries, I'm sure.)

As an amateur, Denaburg ran his heater up into the mid-90s. He combines the fastball with a big hook, and you can see the outlines of an impressive two-pitch mix there. His changeup lags far, far behind, and the command isn't there yet either. There's obviously a lot of reliever risk here until he shows a functional third pitch and durability. 2019 will tell us a lot about what the shape of his career will look like; for now he's an interesting live arm.

The Risks: Maximum. He's a prep arm with reliever risk who spent much of last season dealing with an arm injury. Do I need to say more?

Ben Carsley's Fantasy Take: Bubba Thompson is the Most Rangers prospect, Brendan Rodgers is the Most Rockies Prospect, Kyle Lewis is the Most Mariners prospect, and Denaburg is the Most Nationals prospect. His upside is such that he bears consideration in deeper dynasty leagues—it's not like the Nats haven't gotten the most out of guys like this before—but the risks are high enough that he'll be kept a ways away from the top-101. He'd be in the next 100, though.

5. Yasel Antuna   IF   OFP: 55   Likely: 45   ETA: 2023
Born: 10/26/99   Age: 19   Bats: B   Throws: R   Height: 6'0"   Weight: 170
Origin: International Free Agent, 2016

The Report: The adjective I want to use here is "smooth." He's smooth in the field. He's smooth at the plate. He's a five-tool athlete and things just look easy for him, even if we think he'll grow off shortstop.

You can tell by the statistical line that they weren't easy, obviously. Antuna struggled early and often, and then disappeared to the disabled list for the last six weeks of the season. He assembled a line so bad from the right side of the plate (.165/.252/.214) that it's closer to a decent-hitting pitcher than a bad-hitting hitter.

Indeed, it is the comparison to Garcia that makes Antuna look bad. Consider that Antuna jumped straight out of the complex and didn't face a single pitcher all year that he was older than, and suddenly the season looks okay. Not good, but far from disastrous.

The Risks: High. He might just not hit, and the defensive profile is still unclear. Something intuitively tells me to like him more than I should, though.

Ben Carsley's Fantasy Take: While Kieboom and Garcia may be slightly undervalued fantasy assets, Antuna has been a bit overrated in our circle. The ceiling remains somewhat enticing, and he should be rostered in most TDGX-sized leagues with 200-plus prospects kept, but those in shallower formats can look to players with higher upsides or more favorable ETAs for the time being. Perhaps most damningly, I keep reading his name in Andy Bernard's voice.

6. Seth Romero LHP
OFP: 55　Likely: 45　ETA: 2021
Born: 04/19/96　Age: 23　Bats: L　Throws: L　Height: 6'3"　Weight: 240
Origin: Round 1, 2017 Draft (#25 overall)

The Report: If you're ever sad about your favorite prospect's bad year, just come back and read this blurb. Romero was sent home from spring training due to repeated missed curfews, wasn't assigned to an affiliate until June, suffered an elbow injury while ramping up, and had Tommy John surgery in September after a failed comeback. He was fine if a bit inconsistent when he pitched, still flashing three potential plus offerings: fastball, slider, and changeup. The command was still inconsistent when the injury struck.

Romero repeatedly found trouble before entering pro ball, with publicly-reported incidents and suspensions including more missed curfews, low effort during conditioning drills, a failed marijuana test, and posing with a bong in his uniform. He was ultimately dismissed from his college team for decking a teammate. So the suspension by the Nationals, which we normally wouldn't care much about, is a continuation of an alarming trend. Teams will ultimately ignore this if you can play, of course, but Romero's not there yet. His stock has dropped a lot more than the one spot on this list and half-grade of roles might suggest.

The Risks: Extreme. I usually don't ding guys for makeup without cause, but Romero's now missed large chunks of two straight seasons for tomfoolery. Now he's going to miss another season for Tommy John and, if all goes well, pop back up in 2020 as a 24-year-old with 47⅓ pro innings, all at Low-A or below. You can't stay a top prospect if you're never on the field.

Ben Carsley's Fantasy Take: Does this seem like the type of prospect you really want to invest in? No no, not the bad attitude part—the pitcher with injuries and non-elite upside part? I didn't think so. He and Jon Denney would've made a great battery.

Washington Nationals 2019

7 **Wil Crowe RHP** OFP: 55 Likely: 45
ETA: Late 2019 as a reliever, 2020 as a starter
Born: 09/09/94 Age: 24 Bats: R Throws: R Height: 6'2" Weight: 240
Origin: Round 2, 2017 Draft (#65 overall)

The Report: Crowe started to make up for lost time in 2018—like almost every Nationals pitching prospect, Tommy John is on the resume already—getting to Double-A by the end of his first full professional season. The results were decidedly mixed. Crowe looks like the kind of durable, mid-rotation starter that I have long since run out of new ways to describe in the Annual without resorting to medieval poetic forms. There's above-average fastball velocity, a power slider, a change that needs a grade jump or more, the usual boxes ticked. But Crowe struggled badly at times with his control and command in 2018 and the culprit was not hard to identify. The delivery is extremely high effort and upper-body heavy with late timing. In other words, it all ends up looking more like a 95-and-a-slider relief arm. Given that he's already 24, the Nationals might consider making that conversion sooner rather than later, although getting Crowe more professional innings might take priority for now.

The Risks: Medium. The command and control may wobble too much for him to be effective in the majors even as a reliever. He has a history of arm issues.

Ben Carsley's Fantasy Take: Christ, Daredevil thinks this system fell off quickly.

8 **Jose Sanchez SS** OFP: 55 Likely: 40 ETA: 2023
Born: 07/12/00 Age: 18 Bats: R Throws: R Height: 5'11" Weight: 155
Origin: International Free Agent, 2016

The Report: Here's where the system noticeably thins out. Sanchez is a potential impact defender at the 6, with fantastic instincts and a knack for making the quick and correct first step. We were concerned about his arm some in 2017, but he was playing through an injury and it showed much better in 2018. His hands are strong too, and we're now reasonably confident as 18-year-olds go that he'll stick at shortstop all the way up, and be pretty good there.

The bat… well, if I ever fail to mention a position player's stick in the first paragraph, there's probably a reason. Sanchez has no present power and not much projection. In general, physical projection is the problem here—we're just not seeing it yet. He has some feel for contact, if you want to be nice about things, and he's been extremely young for his levels, so maybe there's more offensively than he's shown so far.

The Risks: Extreme. A lot of things can cause a guy who is a defensively-minded shortstop this low to stop being a defensively-minded shortstop, and not all of them are controllable. He might, for example, just grow a lot more than we think.

Ben Carsley's Fantasy Take: Maybe if he starts hitting or running? Those seem like important qualifiers for fantasy?

9

Tim Cate   LHP   OFP: 50   Likely: 45   ETA: 2021
Born: 09/30/97   Age: 21   Bats: L   Throws: L   Height: 6'0"   Weight: 185
Origin: Round 2, 2018 Draft (#65 overall)

The Report: Cate had first-round buzz coming into the 2018 college season as UCONN's Friday night starter. Working with perhaps the best curveball in the draft class, he began the season well, but the stuff and velocity were a bit inconsistent and he was eventually shut down for "precautionary reasons." Cate returned for the College World Series and the low-90s velocity and 12-6 hammer curve were back. Anyway, the Nats never met a pitcher with questionable medicals who they wouldn't draft, and they popped Cate in the second round.

Cate worked primarily off his fastball as a pro, and the pitch shows some life up with occasional cut. The curve still looks like a plus offering, flashing higher. Cate can manipulate the pitch, and spot or bury it. He doesn't have ideal height, but his near over-the-top slot gives him some plane on his fastball. There isn't much of a changeup here at present, although it dives tantalizingly at times. Cate might be best deployed as a lefty crossover guy out of the pen where he can max out the velo and spam the curve, but the curve might also end up good enough on its own that he can spam it as a starter. He also might get hurt again. Pitchers, man.

The Risks: High. Cate is a shorter lefty without a major-league-quality third pitch and mysterious arm issues in his recent past.

Ben Carsley's Fantasy Take: Can I go home now?

10

Israel Pineda   C   OFP: 50   Likely: 40
ETA: 2024ish? Catchers are weird, man.
Born: 04/03/00   Age: 19   Bats: R   Throws: R   Height: 5'11"   Weight: 190
Origin: International Free Agent, 2016

The Report: Pineda was one of the second-tier prospects the Nationals picked up when they busted their 2016 bonus pool for Antuna, Garcia, and Sanchez. Reports are mixed, but there isn't a lot of offensive impact here at the moment; the bat speed isn't there yet and the present power is muted. If you want to be optimistic, you can point to power potential and some hit tool projectability, and he's hit decently so far. Reports on his glove are stronger, and he has a shot to make the majors as a backup catcher even if he doesn't hit much.

Finding a tenth prospect for this list to replace Daniel Johnson was not fun. You'll see some of the other candidates for that below, and they're not great either. So we're going to go with a high-variance short-season catcher whom we have mixed reports on. It is what it is.

The Risks: High, in the sense that he might not be very good. He's a short-season catcher who we think might be a glove-first backup. He could top out as a Double-A player, or even a Double-A coach.

Ben Carsley's Fantasy Take: Love 2 roster the prospect version of Christian Vazquez for my successful dynasty fantasy baseballing leagues.

Choose Your Own Adventure: Should Any Of These Guys Actually Be 10th?

Two years ago, we had a "pick the tenth-best prospect in the Phillies system" section, because they were so deep that you could make a case for a half-dozen guys at 10. This is, well, the opposite of that—a system bad enough that I was cross-checking names to make sure they didn't declare MILB free agency.

Telmito Agustin, OF

Our first contestant is a 22-year-old hitter from the Virgin Islands. Agustin is a big, strong youngster who we've liked for awhile with the stick, and he hit .300 with some pop as an age-appropriate player in the High-A Carolina League. He runs well and can fake all three outfield spots with varying levels of competence. On the other hand, he's often on the shelf—a dislocated finger cost him almost two months this past summer—and he was just passed up by the 29 other teams in the Rule 5 Draft.

Nick Banks, OF

Bachelor number 2 is a contact-oriented outfielder out of Texas A&M who hasn't made particularly great contact yet. Banks has a nice swing and a decent idea of what he's doing at the plate, but doesn't hit the ball with much authority and probably never will. He does play fine defense at all three outfield spots. This profile passes for interesting in this system because you can see the outline of a defense/contact fourth outfielder or marginal starter here.

Joan Baez, RHP

One of the best-named prospects in baseball, Baez is a fastball/curveball "starter" who throws in the mid-90s and has no idea where anything is going. His command has never taken any kind of leap forward. He has obvious reliever mechanics anyway, with a hard landing and difficulty repeating. The Nationals have stubbornly kept running him out there in various A-ball rotations, although you have to assume the conversion is coming since he still walks five per nine every year. Baez also went unprotected and unpicked in Rule 5.

Jackson Tetreault, RHP

We sort of like Jackson Tetreault and have occasionally touted him as a sleeper. He's a nice get for a JUCO seventh-rounder, a guy with a heavy sinker in the low-90s and a breaking ball that flashes. He had a decent first full campaign in Hagerstown. A reasonable upside projection is a back-of-the-rotation starter or a seventh-inning type reliever, and every system has several pitching prospects of this type. We rarely write them up.

James Bourque, RHP

He has a rockin' mustache! He had a great season in the minors! They actually bothered to put him on the 40-man! He's... ah, crap, it's a 25-year-old reliever in Double-A. Bourque was a struggling starter coming off Tommy John who converted to relief before last season and started getting results off a velocity bump to the mid-90s. He'll probably pitch in the majors in a setup or middle relief role.

Tanner Rainey, RHP

Our last bachelor was plucked out of the Reds system in the Tanner-for-Tanner salary dump. Rainey tops out at 101 MPH and mixes in the exact hard slider you'd expect a guy with that arm strength to throw, also adding in the occasional firm change. That's way better than anyone else we've talked about, right? Well, the kicker is that he turned 26 at the end of December and walked a ton of batters between Triple-A and a few short MLB stints last season.

So, that's how we ended up with a likely backup catcher at the ten-spot...

Top Talents 25 and Under (born 4/1/93 or later):

1. Juan Soto
2. Trea Turner
3. Victor Robles
4. Carter Kieboom
5. Luis Garcia
6. Joe Ross
7. Mason Denaburg
8. Yasel Antuna
9. Koda Glover
10. Seth Romero

Sure, it's a really crappy system. But when you have two young MLBers as good as Soto and Turner, it makes up for a crappy system and then some.

Soto had one of the greatest teenage hitting seasons in the history of baseball. We absolutely adored him as a prospect, even ranking him a spot ahead of Vladito on the 2017 midseason list, and we still didn't see *this* coming. He's already one of the best hitters in baseball and he has another season left before he can legally drink. Enjoy him.

Turner is an above-average hitter, one of the best baserunners in the league, and he's settled in as a capable shortstop after jaunts in center field and second base. 2018 was his first fully-healthy season and he very quietly accrued 5.3 WARP. If he can keep playing every day, we'd expect him to have a few seasons where he contends for batting titles and MVPs.

Surprisingly, Joe Ross is still eligible for this list. He emerged as a quality mid-rotation starter way back in 2015 but missed most of the past two seasons recovering from Tommy John. He was injury-prone even before the surgery, so we're not fantastically optimistic that he's ever going to be a consistent 30-start guy. If your glass is half full, his stuff did look pretty much normal in a September cameo, and he used his changeup as a third pitch far more than in the past.

I don't have the slightest idea what to do with Koda Glover, who came back late in the season from shoulder surgery without his best fastball. I think the slider is still good enough for late-inning relief, but he turns 26 right after Opening Day and between injuries and underperformance, he's yet to establish himself in the majors.

Part 3: Featured Articles

The Hole in The Shift is Fixing Itself

Russell Carleton

I've been on a bit of a mission against The Shift of late. I'm not out to get The Shift for the usual reasons that people oppose it. The words "the right way to play the game" won't be found on my lips. If a team wants to pursue a strategy that is within the rules and it works, then by all means, they have my blessing (not that they need it). Instead, my concern with The Shift is a worry that it doesn't work, or at least that it has a flaw that needs fixing.

The data show that while The Shift does a decent job of preventing singles on balls in play (what it's supposed to do), it also increases the number of walks that happen in front of it, and the number of additional walks outweighs the number of singles saved. It's a problem because you can't throw a guy out if he gets to walk to first base.

But the "why" was important. It seemed that The Shift was changing the way in which pitchers pitched. We saw that there were fewer fastballs thrown in front of The Shift than we might otherwise expect, and that pitchers tended to stay out of the strike zone a little more. Not by a lot. In fact, it might not even be visible to the naked eye. The percentage of pitches that are out of the zone goes from 51.0 to 53.3 from a standard defense (two right/two left) to a full shift (three on one side). That difference stands up even after we control for the types of hitters that get shifted against. And it's enough to drive up the walk rate to where it cancels out the benefits that teams thought they were getting with The Shift... and then some.

But there was some hope. I found that when individual pitchers stayed closer to the in-zone/out-of-zone mix that they used without The Shift on, they could still get the benefits of The Shift without the walk problems. So, in theory, a team could simply figure out a way to convince its pitchers to not fall prey to the walk trap and The Shift would once again be their friend.

It's reasonable to think that some teams might be more hip to this idea than others. Maybe some figured it out a year before the others. Maybe they were better at getting the message across to their pitchers. Or, maybe no one has figured it out yet.

Warning! Gory Mathematical Details Ahead!

I used data from 2015-2017, made available through MLB's data portal, Baseball Savant. They are kind enough to note when teams are using an infield shift (three fielders on one side of second base), as opposed to a "strategic shift" (someone's playing a bit out of position, but it's not quite that drastic) or a "standard" alignment.

Since we're doing this by team, I can't just look at raw walk rates, because we know that some teams have good pitchers and others have not-so-good pitchers. Some have a mix of both. I used the log-odds ratio method to take into account a batter's general walking proclivities, and a pitcher's as well, and then shoving them into a binary logistic regression. Then, I asked the computer to generate a specific coefficient for each team's pitchers, for when they went into The Shift and how that affected their walk rate.

Using those coefficients, I was able to project what would happen if a league-average pitcher faced a league-average hitter (which we expect would product a league-average walk rate; from 2015-2017, 7.7 percent of plate appearances ended in a walk) and then just switched his hat. Here's the top five and the bottom five:

Top 5 Teams	Projected Shift Walk Rate	Bottom 5 Teams	Projected Shift Walk Rate
Rockies	6.2%	Rangers	11.2%
Pirates	6.7%	Mets	10.4%
Indians	7.2%	Dodgers	10.2%
Astros	7.3%	Cardinals	9.9%
Braves	7.7%	Tigers	9.7%

There are probably people out there right now trying to figure out what the common thread is among the top and bottom teams. I'm sure, because this is Baseball Prospectus, people are already trying to make the case that sabermetric "early adopters" have some sort of edge here. I think that the more interesting piece is that by the time you get to fifth place in The Shift, we're at league average.

As a sanity check, I examined the issue on a pitch-by-pitch level, looking at how often pitchers threw their pitches in the GameDay strike zone, and again using the same basic methodology and getting team-specific coefficients. The names on the list re-arranged themselves, but the idea was the same, and the two lists correlated with an R of .593.

There's a reason that I don't usually do this type of leaderboard post. I don't really know what the Rockies, Pirates, Indians, Astros, and Braves have in common, or what they have that the bottom five don't. I can put a shrug emoji here and say, "Well, it must be something!" but that seems like a cop-out. Instead, I'd like to present another table and suggest that the table above doesn't even really matter anymore.

Year	League Percent Outside K Zone (Full Shift)	League Percent in K Zone (No Shift)	Difference
2015	54.1%	51.1%	3.0%
2016	53.3%	50.9%	2.4%
2017	52.6%	50.9%	1.7%
2018	52.0%	50.7%	1.3%

The hole in The Shift is fixing itself, and it's coming down really fast league wide. In my earlier work on The Shift, I suggested that until teams stopped having such a huge difference between their out-of-zone rate with and without The Shift on, there would just be too many walks for The Shift to make sense. It seems that all 30 of them have been working toward just that. I once estimated that it takes about 10 years for an idea to filter its way through baseball. At this rate, it looks like teams are going to catch up a lot faster than that. And yeah, they're all saber-smart now.

It's likely that whatever magic it was that the Rockies and Pirates had has made its way to Texas and Queens. Or is at least on its way. And if teams are committing to fixing the walk problem, then it's likely that they will continue shifting and shifting a lot.

And eventually it's going to actually make sense for them to do it.

—*Russell Carleton is a former author of Baseball Prospectus and now an analyst for the New York Mets.*

The State of the Quality Start

Rob Mains

One of the seven things you (probably) didn't know about the 2018 season is that quality starts—defined as a start lasting six or more innings with three or fewer earned runs allowed—as a percentage of total starts cratered to an all-time low of 41 percent. I want to look a little more deeply into this, since it's been a while (May of 2016, to be exact) since I've examined quality starts.

The term *quality start* is credited to *Philadelphia Inquirer* sportswriter John Lowe. It's been derided ever since he coined it in December of 1985. Three runs in six innings? That's a 4.50 ERA! In what world is that a measure of quality?

Let's start with that criticism. It's true that 3 x 9 / 6 = 4.5. (You came here for this sort of high-level math, right?) But it's also true that type of start, meeting the bare minimum for earning a quality start, is unusual. Here's the proportion of quality starts in which the pitcher lasted exactly six innings and yielded exactly three earned runs. (I'm going to confine this analysis to the 30-team era, 1998-present. Almost all data retrieved in this article is via the Baseball-Reference Play Index.)

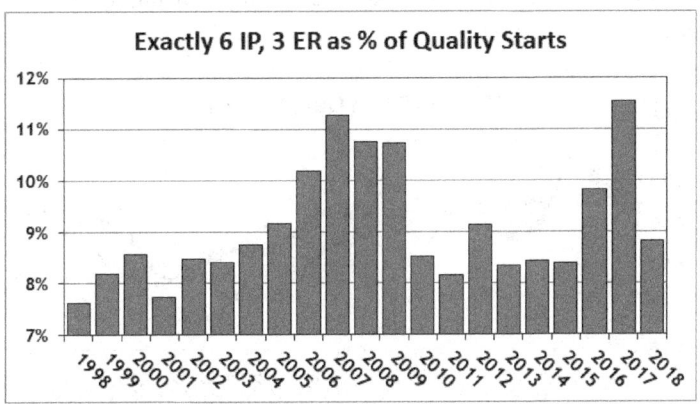

There were 1,997 quality starts in 2018. Only 176, or fewer than one in 11, featured a pitcher going six innings and allowing three earned runs. Put another way, the percentage of quality starts that resulted in a 4.50 ERA (8.8 percent) is less than half the percentage of games in which a batter hit two home runs and his team lost (22.5 percent; 237-69 won-lost). That doesn't impugn hitting two homers.

So if a 4.50 ERA isn't the norm, what is? How good are quality starts?

Pretty good, it turns out. First, on a team level:

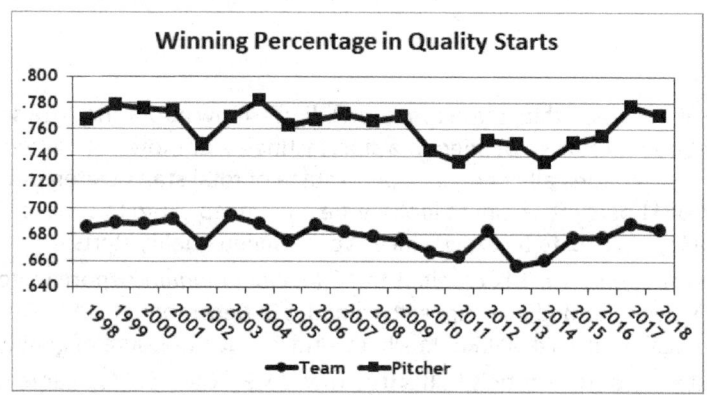

Teams receiving a quality start from their pitcher won 68.4 percent of their games in 2018, in line with the 30-team era average of 67.9 percent. A team with a .684 winning percentage wins 111 games. Getting a quality start is definitely a good thing. Individual pitchers throwing quality starts have a higher winning percentage because a big slice of team losses is assigned to a reliever.

If teams do well in quality starts, how well do the starting pitchers do? Again, very well.

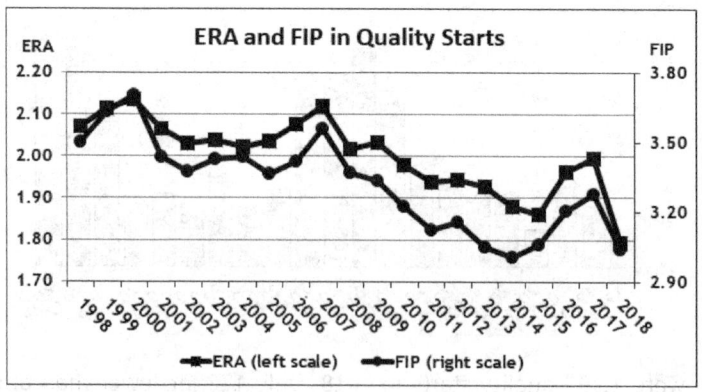

Pitchers in quality starts had a 1.79 ERA (blue line) in 2018, *the lowest in the 30-team era*. Their FIP was higher, 3.04, but still excellent. In the 30-team era, only 2014 had a lower FIP for quality starts, 3.01.

But, of course, the run environment in 2014 was different. Teams in 2014 scored 4.07 runs per game, the fewest in a non-strike year since 1976. They scored 4.45 runs per game in 2018. So surrendering a 3.04 FIP in 2018 is more impressive than 3.01 in 2014. Accordingly, let's look at ERA and FIP in quality starts relative to league averages.

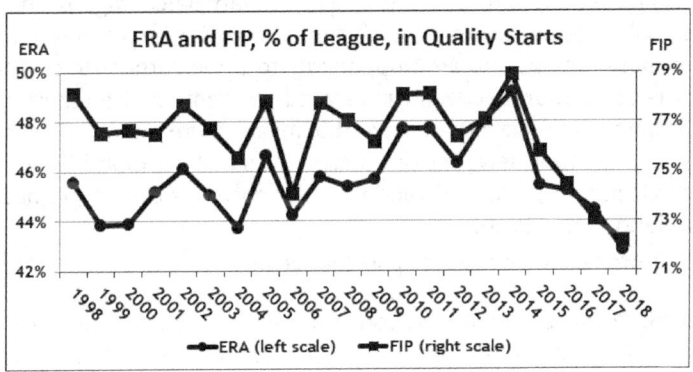

This tells a more dramatic story. Starting pitchers in 2018 gave up a 4.19 ERA and a 4.21 FIP. Starters in quality starts gave up a 1.79 ERA, 43 percent of the league average. Starters in quality starts gave up a 3.04 FIP, 72 percent of the league average. Both of these marks represent lows in the 30-team era.

The takeaway here is this: *Quality starts are better, relative to other starts, than they've ever been over the past 21 years.*

Maybe during the winter I'll look at this over a longer arc of time. For now, though, we can definitively say quality starts are the best they've ever been since the Diamondbacks and Rays joined the majors.

Yet, paradoxically, they're down.

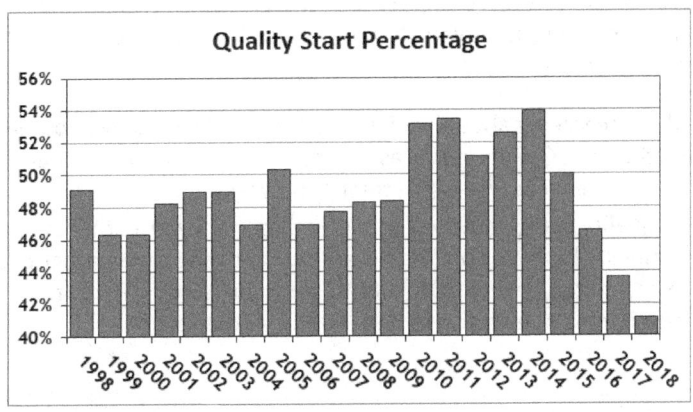

This graph covers only the 30-team era. In my article last week, though, I looked at the years 1908-2018. The result was the same. The 41 percent of starts in 2018 that were quality starts are an all-time low, well below the runners-up: 1930's 43 percent (the year teams scored an all-time record 5.55 runs per game) and last year's 44 percent.

The normal explanation for a dip in quality start percentage is an increase in scoring. When teams score a lot of runs, it's harder for starting pitchers to last six or more innings and limit opponents to three earned runs. From 1998 to 2014, the correlation between runs scored per game and the percentage of starts that were quality starts was -0.94. That means there was an extremely close relationship: More runs, fewer quality starts. Too small a sample? Go back to the start of the Expansion Era, 1961, and the relationship is even more negative, a -0.95 correlation, though 2014.

But that's broken down over the past four years:

- 2015: Runs per game increased from 4.07 to 4.25, quality start percentage decreased from 54.0 to 50.1. Yes, that's a negative relationship, but the regression model would predict a decline of 1.5 percentage points. We got 3.9 instead.
- 2016: Runs per game increased from 4.25 to 4.48, quality start percentage decreased from 50.1 to 46.6. Past experience would suggest a decline of just 1.8 percentage points. We got 3.4.
- 2017: Runs per game increased from 4.48 to 4.65, quality start percentage decreased from 46.6 to 43.6. Again, the direction's right, but the magnitude isn't. Using the relationship from 1998 to 2014, that increase in scoring should've reduced quality starts by 1.3 percentage points, not 2.9.
- 2018: Runs per game declined from 4.65 to 4.45. That should've resulted in the quality start percentage moving in the other direction, rising 1.6 points. It didn't. It fell 2.6 points, as noted, to an all-time low.

Granted, we're talking about just four years here. Maybe they're outliers. But I don't think they are. Quality starts, as noted, are as good or better than ever. But they're rarer than ever as well. And I think I know why.

To get a quality start, you need to allow three or fewer earned and pitch at least six innings. That's 18 outs. Here's a graph showing the number of starting pitchers who limited their opponents to three or fewer earned runs but got pulled after pitching at least five innings but fewer than six:

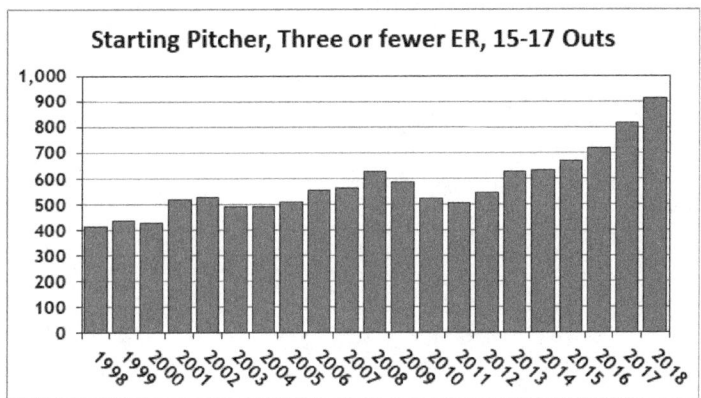

A pitcher getting 15 outs pitched five innings. A pitcher getting 16 outs pitched 5 1/3. A pitcher getting 17 outs pitched 5 2/3. More than ever before, pitchers are being removed from games in which they are within 1-3 outs of a quality start, falling just short of the six-inning finish line. Widespread acknowledgement of the times-through-the-order penalty and a flotilla of available bullpen arms is making the quality start simultaneously both more excellent and more rare.

Which is ironic, given that we saw a new post-war quality start record this season:

Rank	Pitcher	Season	Consecutive QS
1	Jacob deGrom	2018	24
2	Bob Gibson	1968	22
-	Chris Carpenter	2005	22
4	Johan Santana	2004	21
5	Luis Tiant	1968	20
-	Mike Scott	1986	20
-	Jake Arrieta	2015	20
8	Robin Roberts	1952	19
-	Tom Seaver	1973	19
-	Jack Morris	1983	19
-	Greg Maddux	1998	19
-	Josh Johnson	2010	19
-	Jon Lester	2014	19

While there have been longer streaks spread over multiple seasons, no pitcher since World War II threw more consecutive quality starts in one year than Jacob deGrom this year. The fact that he did in a year in which quality starts were the rarest they've ever been adds to the accomplishment.

—*Rob Mains is an author of Baseball Prospectus.*

Heads-Up Hacking—The First Pitch

Matthew Trueblood

Batters fell behind in a higher percentage of all plate appearances in 2018 than in any previous season for which we have pitch-by-pitch data. That kind of granular information goes back only to 1988, but we might safely assume (given all we know about baseball as it had been before that, and as it has been in the years since) that batters have *never* fallen behind at a higher rate than they did last season.

Through the 1990s, the percentage of all plate appearances that began 0-1 hovered in the high 30s and low 40s. In the 2000s, it rose steadily but slowly, through the mid-40s. In 2018, 49.8 percent of all trips to the plate began 0-1. That, as much as anything, captures in microcosm the nature of hitting in MLB today.

A countdown clock toward strike three begins ticking almost the moment a batter takes his place in the box. The league's adjusted OPS+ on the first pitch was higher in 2018 than ever before, and that has been true in most of the last 10 seasons. Batters hit .264/.289/.442 in all plate appearances in which they swung at the first pitch last season, and .241/.330/.395 in all plate appearances in which they took that first offering.

The percentage differences in batting average and isolated power there favor swinging at the first pitch by more than in any season since 1988, while the difference in on-base percentage favors taking by more than ever. If you want to get on base at a decent clip, it's a good idea to be patient, but you run the risk of missing the only chances you'll get to produce power.

Washington Nationals 2019

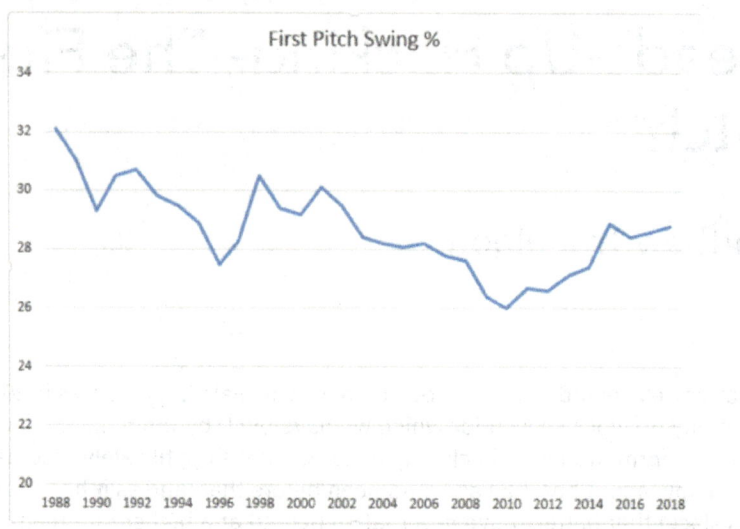

The league swung at the first pitch 28.8 percent of the time in 2018. With the isolated exception of 2015, that's the highest that number has climbed since 2002, but it might not be high enough. With the help of BP research maven Rob McQuown, I looked at the aggregate Called Strike Probability (CSProb) on the first pitch for each season since 2008, when the implementation of PITCHf/x first made measuring that possible. It's risen sharply during that period.

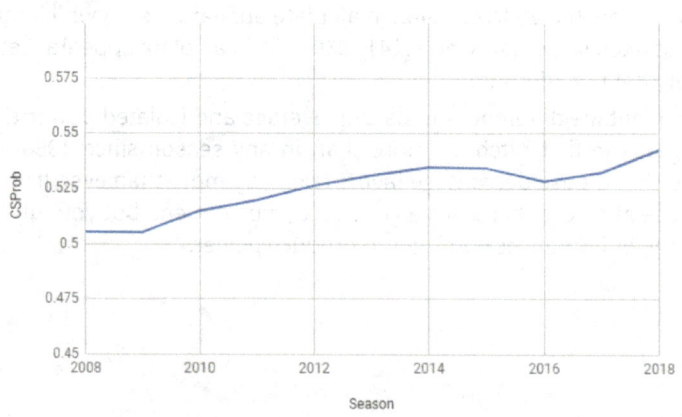

Called Strike Probability, First Pitch of PA (2008-2018)

Called Strike Probability is exactly what it sounds like: a pitch with a given CSProb has roughly that chance of being called a strike, if not swung at. In 2018, a batter who took 100 first pitches from a random sampling of the league's pitchers might expect to fall behind 54 or 55 times—up from 50 or 51 times in 2008. Almost regardless of pitch type (and, notably, especially in the case of fastballs), the first pitch tends to have more of the zone right now than ever before.

Pitchers are better at throwing strikes. They have better stuff, and believe more in their ability to miss bats within the zone. Perhaps most importantly, they know that batters are looking for one thing on the first pitch: a fastball. If they don't get it, they're likely to take the pitch. Check out how the use of sinkers and four-seamers on the first pitch has changed in a decade:

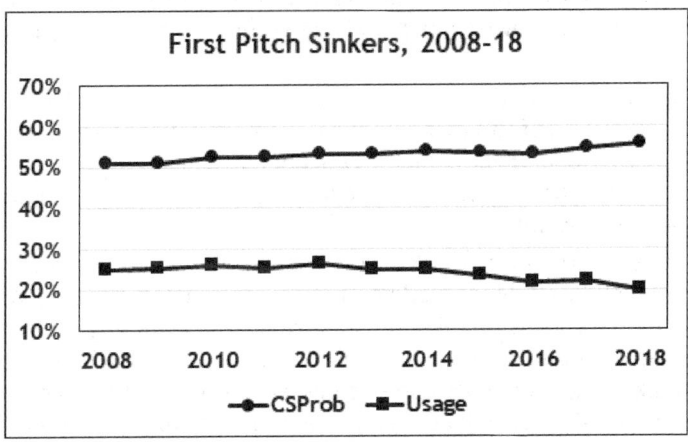

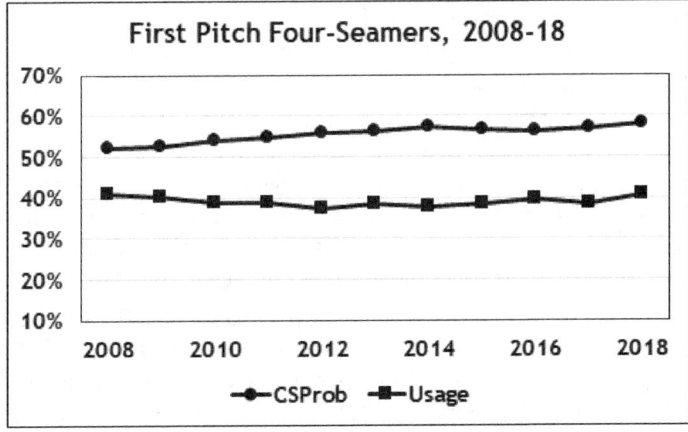

The sinker is losing its place in baseball, but the rate at which pitchers have thrown it on the first pitch hasn't dropped any faster than its usage rate in other counts. Pitchers have actually gone to their four-seamer *more* often to open counts, in the last few years, after a dip in the 2012-2015 period. What's really changed, though, and what shows up in both charts above, is that pitchers are catching more of the zone with first-pitch fastballs than they were a decade ago, or a half-decade ago. They're attacking right away, even with the pitch they know batters are expecting. The message is pretty clear: batters are being too passive.

Sliders, curves, and changeups each have more of the zone when thrown on the first pitch than they did several years ago, too, though the effect is less pronounced. Pitchers have seen the numbers; they know batters are doing better on the first pitch itself. They still feel safe throwing more and better strikes than ever before, figuring they'll come out ahead as long as they keep getting ahead to open each battle.

The Moneyball revolution brought an increased league-wide focus on OBP, which resulted in a de facto mandate to take a more patient tack at the plate. It worked very well for a while, as batters with poor plate discipline were compelled to either adjust or be expelled from the league, and pitchers with poor control were slowly weeded out.

However, concurrent with that revolution, and spurred by it in some ways, was the evolution of the pitching paradigm that now dominates the game. As batters ratcheted up their focus on inflating pitch counts and working walks, pitchers honed theirs on throwing strikes and missing bats. The league's understanding of what makes a good pitcher improved at least as much, from the mid-1990s through the mid-2000s, as its understanding of what makes a good hitter. As amphetamines and other performance-enhancing drugs were phased mostly out of the game, and as PITCHf/x broke onto the scene, individuals and teams learned how to exploit the evolved approaches of even the smartest hitters.

The ability to avoid making outs is still the most valuable one in baseball, but the magnitude of its eclipse of slugging is smaller than ever. To a greater extent than power, on-base skills derive their value from chaining—from the on-base skill levels of the players on either side of a given individual. Eleven years ago, when the housing crisis hit, people learned the hard way that the value of their homes depended a good deal on the values of their neighbors' homes. The same wasn't true, though, of their cars. So it is now, with OBP and SLG.

The global OBP in 2018 was .318. The only seasons since the Dead Ball Era in which the league got on base at a worse clip were 2013-2015, 1988, 1971-1972, and 1963-1968. This is all happening despite the aforementioned evolution of the science of hitting. It's happening despite a shift in approach and focus, one that would steer OBP ever higher, if only it were working.

Instead, it's sitting at a low ebb, and while it does so, even guys who get on base often are a little less helpful than they were 10 years ago—or 20, or 40, or 60, or 70, or 80, or 90. They're less helpful, that is, because unless there happen to be three or four other guys in the lineup who get on just as regularly, their contribution is merely to forestall the inevitable. Runs happen, increasingly, when a sudden bang happens, and that means attacking early in the count—because pitchers are sure as hell doing that.

In a league making contact on barely 75 percent of its swings, and a league in which an increasing number of pitchers can throw multiple off-speed pitches for strikes in any count, the only way to consistently generate offense is going to be aggressive. This isn't necessarily true for individuals, like Mookie Betts and Jose Ramirez, who make a lot of contact and have excellent plate discipline, and whose power comes from such natural quickness in a short stroke. Most players have to make tradeoffs, though, whether it be lowering their contact rate or raising their chase rate, in order to consistently make the quality of contact necessary to survive in today's game.

Highest %	Lowest %
Javier Baez – 48.3	Joe Mauer – 4.6
Freddie Freeman – 47.1	Mookie Betts – 9.7
Ozzie Albies – 46.3	Brett Gardner – 10.7
Jose Altuve – 44.2	Jose Ramirez – 12.0
Nick Castellanos – 44.1	Jason Kipnis – 13.8
Joey Gallo – 42.3	Jesus Aguilar – 14.5
Corey Dickerson – 40.9	Xander Bogaerts – 15.8
Salvador Perez – 40.8	Brian Dozier – 16.3
Eddie Rosario – 40.7	Mike Trout – 17.6
Nick Ahmed – 40.4	Yasmani Grandal – 17.6

Top 10 and Bottom 10 Hitters, First-Pitch Swing Rate (2018)

The question isn't which of these lists one prefers, but what they each convey, qualitatively, about the cat-and-mouse game of early-count hitting. Those top five on the left, especially, drive home the fact that for most players, getting aggressive early in the count is now key to keeping strikeout rate down and hitting for power.

For now, the message is: pitchers are coming right after batters with the nastiest stuff they've ever had. Batters had better stop giving away strike one and force hurlers to adjust, or the global OBP crisis is only going to get worse.

—*Matthew Trueblood is an author of Baseball Prospectus.*

A Hymn for the Index Stat

Patrick Dubuque

We survived without computers. I know this, because I remember the day when my dad hooked up his brand-new Atari 400 computer to the back of our 12-inch Magnavox television, and the perfect blue of the memo pad lit up for the first time. I was born just on the edge of that transitional generation, of learning cursive and balancing checkbooks and just doing math all the time, constant manual arithmetic.

It still amazes me. We learned how to sail ships without computers. We learned how to do calculus. We built towers that didn't fall down, most of the time. We engineered catapults to knock them down anyway. We built a robust system of philosophy called "utilitarianism," founded on the principle that the good of an action is evaluated by summing the effects of that action, which is the kind of formula that would make the world's mainframes crash. The whole foundation of statistics as a field is "here's math you could easily do but would die of old age first."

The fact of the matter is that there is too much math in the world to do. There are too many things changing, and too many things too small to notice, for us to handle. At some point, they become too much for the computers to handle as well, which is why we have chaos theory and undetectable earthquakes, but it's not an even fight. At some point, we fall back on intuition, and given how under-equipped we are, we're forced to bestow that intuition with some sort of supernatural superiority, the "gut feeling," that we can't prove because we can only intuit that our intuition is better.

We're all lousy at intuition, and wonderful at lying to ourselves about it. The honest truth is that computers are far better at intuition than we are, because in order to know what feels "off" you have to know what's "on." In order to do that you have to constantly reassess the average of everything, then re-rank your own experience against it.

Test your own, by comparing these three anonymous lines:

Player	G	HR	AVG	OBP	SLG
Player A	156	38	.259	.342	.535
Player B	154	38	.280	.348	.527
Player C	158	38	.266	.343	.509

These all seem like pretty similar players, right? The second one a touch more batted-ball dependent, the third a little less strong, but all pretty good hitters. And you'd be right, about the latter. Not the former.

Here's the breakdown:

- Player A: 1991 Howard Johnson, 141 DRC+
- Player B: 1996 Dean Palmer, 121 DRC+
- Player C: 2018 Giancarlo Stanton, 114 DRC+

Baseball is fortunate to have escaped the seismic shifts of so many other sports, where the talents and performances of other eras are nearly unrecognizable. (And not just other sports: try to explain the greatness of the movie Duck Soup without adjusting for era.) But they're still there, and they're nearly impossible to account for manually, without having to resort to sweeping generalizations like "steroid era" or juiced-ball era" to throw out entire swathes of production.

This is all to say that we should celebrate the index stat, that simple 100-based scale with such a humble aim: just to give context. It's hard to imagine how we lived without them for so long. Sabermetricians have always tried to make their stats look like other stats: True Average mapped to batting average, FIP molded to look like and compare to ERA. It's easy to understand the motivation—these statistics carry an emotional value in them that is hard to resist, as with the .300 hitter and the 2.00 ERA—but even they fall prey to the same loss of scale as their unadjusted counterparts. If a .300 average means different things in different years, does that hold true for a .300 True Average?

Instead, 100 doesn't say anything, except above average or below. And it does it instantly, for every season in every run environment for any statistic we want it to. We should have more index stats: K%+, so we can stop comparing Mike Clevinger's career 9.46 K/9 to Nolan Ryan's 9.55. HBP%+, so we can note that Ron Hunt was getting plunked when nobody else was getting plunked, as opposed to that imitator Brandon Guyer. Some might note how stale these references are and accuse league-adjustment as a backward-looking drive, and this is true. But we're always looking backward, always comparing the new with the expectations already set. The index stat just forces us to be honest.

There's always resistance to a new statistic, especially one so outwardly simple and so internally complex. We tend to stick with what we know, even in the case of formulas that are supposed to tell us what we know. But if your resistance is that it seems too complicated, too counterintuitive, too "black boxy," I encourage you to consider why you feel that way. Because the real world is infinitely more complicated than baseball, where all the pitches go in one basic direction and the baserunners are only allowed to travel in four directions. Baseball statistics based on mixed methodology are almost impossibly intricate. So are skyscrapers and automobiles. That's why we have computers—to take the guesswork out of them.

—*Patrick Dubuque is an author of Baseball Prospectus.*

Index of Names

Acevedo, Carlos 95
Adams, Austin 87
Adams, Matt 20
Agustin, Telmito 94, 104
Antuna, Yasel 94, 100
Baez, Joan 104
Banks, Nick 104
Barraclough, Kyle 50
Bautista, Rafael 81
Bourque, James 105
Canning, Gage 82
Cate, Tim 88, 103
Condra-Bogan, Jacob 95
Corbin, Patrick 52
Cordero, Jimmy 95
Crowe, Wil 89, 102
Denaburg, Mason 90, 100
Diaz, Geraldi 94
Difo, Wilmer 22
Doolittle, Sean 54
Dozier, Brian 24
Eaton, Adam 26
Fedde, Erick 56
Garcia, Luis 83, 99
Glover, Koda 58
Gomes, Yan 28
Grace, Matt 60
Hellickson, Jeremy 62
Hernandez, Alfonso 95
Kendrick, Howie 30
Kieboom, Carter 84, 98
Kieboom, Spencer 32
McGowin, Kyle 95
Miller, Justin 64
Nuno, Vidal 95
Pineda, Israel 103
Rainey, Tanner 66, 105
Read, Raudy 85
Rendon, Anthony 34
Reynolds, Matt 94
Robles, Victor 36, 97
Romero, Jhon 95
Romero, Seth 91, 101
Rosenthal, Trevor 92
Ross, Joe 68
Sanchez, Adrian 94
Sanchez, Anibal 70
Sanchez, Jose 102
Scherzer, Max 72
Severino, Pedro 38
Sharp, Sterling 95
Sipp, Tony 75
Soto, Juan 40
Stevenson, Andrew 94
Strasburg, Stephen 77
Suero, Wander 79
Suzuki, Kurt 42
Taylor, Chuck 94
Taylor, Michael 44
Tetreault, Jackson 95, 104
Turner, Trea 46
Upshaw, Armond 94

Voth, Austin 95
Ward, Drew 86
Williams, Austen 93
Wiseman, Rhett 94
Zimmerman, Ryan 48

Ballpark diagrams for Baseball Prospectus are created by THIRTY81Project, a design concept offering original ballpark artwork, including the new 'Ballparks of 2019' 11 x 17 color print.

Visit **www.thirty81project.com** for full details.

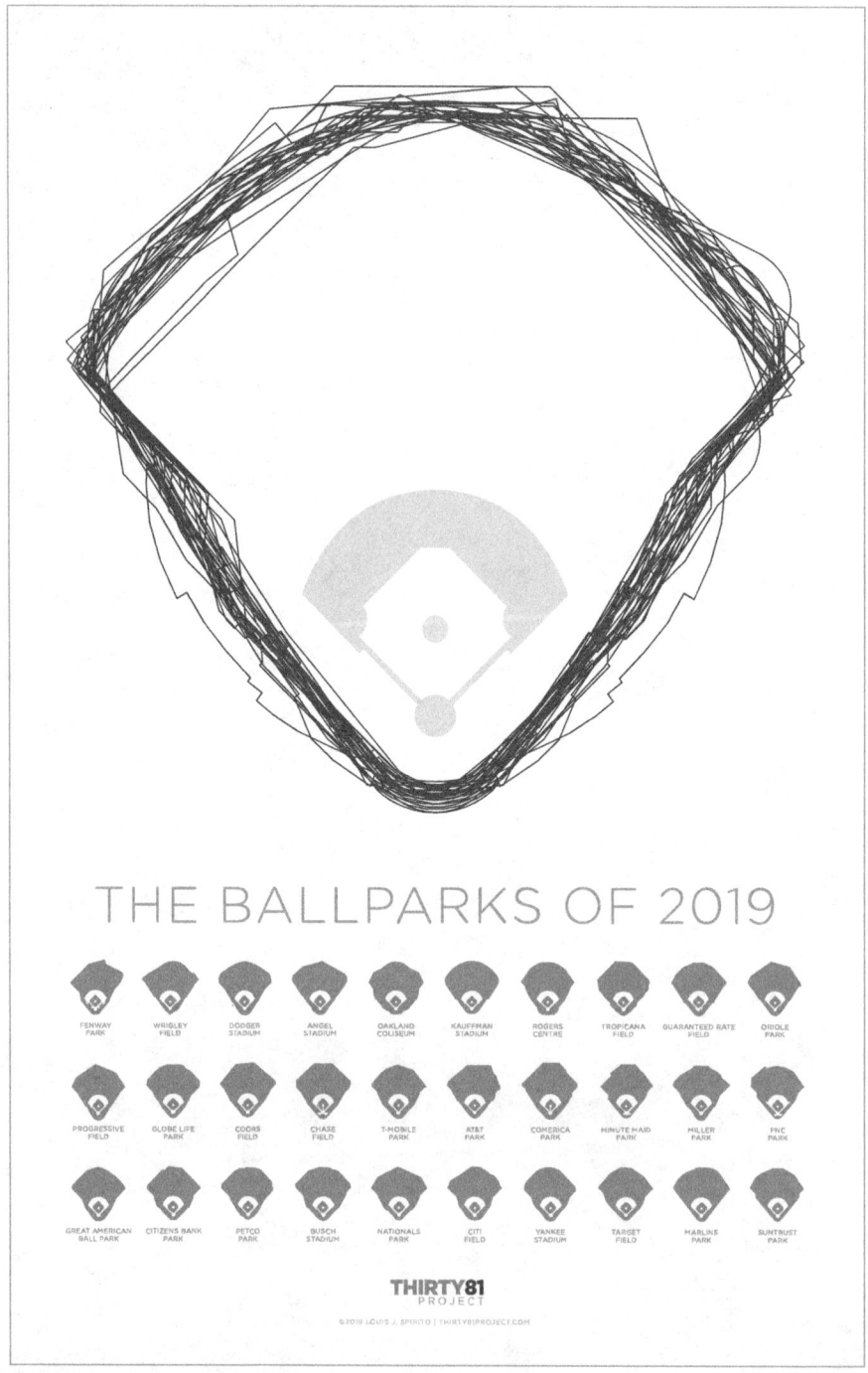